Passing Your Weak Subjects

Ideal for students of any subject, this highly accessible and practical study guide gives you quick and easy strategies to help you make decisive progress in the subjects you find difficult or uninteresting, leaving you free to concentrate on the subjects you love.

Richard Palmer draws on his extensive experience of secondary school teaching to:

- give proven subject-specific advice that will help students from 15–19;
- show you how to understand more about a topic through both online and traditional study;
- help you get to grips with topics you find difficult without cramming you with random facts;
- provide top tips for the essentials to learn and understand on a subject-by-subject basis.

The book is organised to take you through the learning process from 'Facing it' to 'Enjoying it' – yes, that's right!

The author's light-hearted yet authoritative style makes this book really easy to read and his simple and practical advice will enable you to become a confident learner in no time at all.

Richard Palmer is Director of General Education at Bedford School. His other Routledge titles include *Getting Straight 'A's, Studying for Success, The Good Grammar Guide* and *Write in Style*.

Passing Your Weak Subjects

You are much better than you think!

Richard Palmer

Routledge
Taylor & Francis Group

LONDON AND NEW YORK

First published 2008
by Routledge
2 Park Square, Milton Park, Abingdon OX14 4RN

Simultaneously published in the USA and Canada
by Routledge
270 Madison Avenue, New York, NY 10016

*Routledge is an imprint of the Taylor & Francis Group,
an informa business*

© 2008 Richard Palmer

Typeset in Galliard and Gill Sans by
Florence Production Ltd, Stoodleigh, Devon
Printed and bound in Great Britain by
TJ International Ltd, Padstow, Cornwall

British Library Cataloguing in Publication Data
A catalogue record for this book is available from the British Library

Library of Congress Cataloging in Publication Data
Palmer, Richard, 1947–
  Passing your weak subjects: you are much better than
  you think/Richard Palmer.
    p. cm. – (Routledge study guides)
    Includes bibliographical references and index.
  1. Study skills. 2. Education – Curricula. I. Title.
  LB1049.P354 2008
  371.3028′1—dc22   2007051021

ISBN 10: 0–415–40470–3 (hbk)
ISBN 10: 0–415–40471–1 (pbk)
ISBN 10: 0–203–89510–X (ebk)

ISBN 13: 978–0–415–40470–9 (hbk)
ISBN 13: 978–0–415–40471–6 (pbk)
ISBN 13: 978–0–203–89510–8 (ebk)

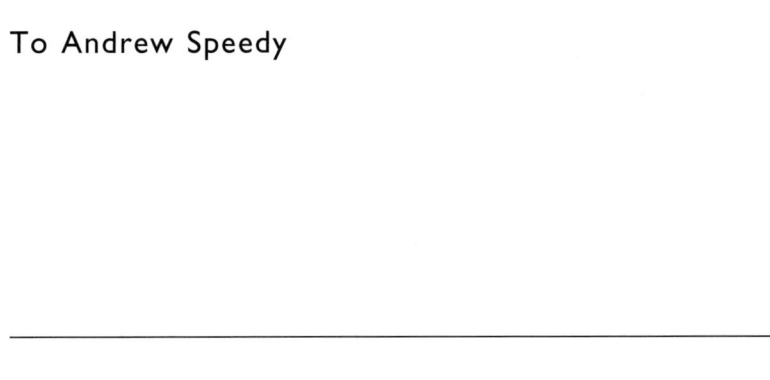

To Andrew Speedy

Contents

Acknowledgements

First, I am immensely grateful to my Commissioning Editor, Philip Mudd; he believed in this book and put up with my year-long-plus delay in delivering it. Much the same applies to his no less excellent and long-suffering Manuscript Editor, Lucy Wainwright.

I must also – joyously – thank the following colleagues and friends, who have directly or indirectly fed what follows. Alan Detweiler, who loaned me his Toronto penthouse flat where eighty per cent of this book was written; Ann Palmer, without whose love and support I would never have written anything; David Ashton, my new English boss at Bedford School; Tim Kirkup; all Bedford School English colleagues past and present, especially David Cundall and dedicatee Andrew Speedy, and 'externals' – Colin Marsh, Ian Sheldon, Michael and Louise Tucker, and Linda Caldicott. Additional thanks to Charles, Edward and Heather Turnham, and to Phil Young and William Young – separated by forty years, but both equally majestic.

Above all, my thanks to Bedford School's Heads of Department (see Appendix III) and all my Bedford School pupils across nearly a quarter of a century. The latter taught me a great deal of what I know and have, therefore, attempted to propagate, in what follows.

Preface

This is my fifth title in Routledge's *Study Guides* Series, and I count myself truly fortunate to say so. The fourth was *Getting Straight 'A's*, published in 2006; almost immediately upon its appearance and reception, my splendid editor Philip Mudd suggested I write a parallel or companion text for those who found academic study rather less easy at times than those whom I 'targeted' in that fourth book.

All of which is worth, perhaps needs, some further explanation and exploration. I much enjoyed writing *Getting Straight 'A's*; it came quickly and, insofar as any assiduous author can say such a thing, easily. But it struck me, during its composition and after its appearance, that there was something a mite strange about writing a 'Study Guide' for those who are Gifted & Talented. That term needs immediate focus before I move on to the core of the rationale for this latest book.

'Gifted & Talented' is a buzz term that reminds me, very much, of a marvellous remark coined by Ian Fleming (in the person of Tiffany Case) in his *Diamonds Are Forever*:

> It reads better than it lives.

Not to grandstand, but aside from my mainstream activities as teacher, lecturer and writer, I am, from time to time, an ISI Inspector – that is to say, the Independent Sector's equivalent of Ofsted. I have done nine such inspections, and by the time you read these words, I will have done a tenth. I and my various (excellent) colleagues do not do it for the money: for reasons you probably wouldn't be interested in anyway and which would waste our valuable joint-study time, I receive £100 – and it's not even tax-free! We do it because we believe in inspections as consultancies, as a way of enabling fine (in my privileged experience, usually superb) schools to become even better.

All that said and sincerely meant, no school that I've visited or inspected or read about has even begun to understand what 'Gifted & Talented' means, let alone put in place programmes that mobilise that concept. Nobody, from government downwards (some might mischievously say 'upwards'), has worked out the criteria by which 'G & T' might be codified – including wondering if it should be a solely academic matter. David Beckham is – or at least was – G & T; so are Ant & Dec; likewise Terry Wogan, in his many media guises over forty years; likewise, too, such diverse but unquestionably classy, even genius-level talents as Andrew Flintoff, Roger Federer, Judi Dench, Andrew Marr, Ian McEwan, Helena Bonham-Carter, Clint Eastwood. Even Bruce Forsyth (astounding talent, even if some of its manifestations are less than enlightening) and Jerry Springer, Oprah Winfrey and Jeremy Clarkson (same remarks apply).

What constitutes 'Gifts'? What does 'Talent' mean? Virtually anything and everything – which is *wonderful*: a fundamental observation about, and tribute to, the genius implicit in our very *Homo sapiens* species.

And so to the rationale that informs this latest title of mine. It is – finally – *easy* to do the things you do if you happen to be G & T. That does not mean you don't have to work at it, and constantly; however, because you're so good at it, that work is a pleasure rather than toil. It is nothing like so easy – or, apparently, easy *at all* – to prosper in things that do not come easily, or which you think are not 'you', or, even, which you think just stink.

Wrong! You might think you are rubbish at this, that or the other; you are not. All you need to do is approach your alleged weaknesses, blind-spots, everything that drives you either crazy or into sapping depression, with affirmation, confidence and determination. Or, to put it another way: hit the vanity button! As my subtitle announces – and I mean it, with both intellectual conviction and passionate belief – *you are much better than you think!* Accept that for starters, and you've already taken the first few – and vital – steps – not only to 'pass' your weak subjects, but very possibly to triumph at them.

Chapter 1

Facing it
The facts

Some governing observations

- Even at its least inspired, the human brain is a miraculous instrument. Its full potential is, if not infinite, more or less incalculable; it is laughably superior to the most sophisticated computer ever imagined, let alone manufactured; it is the greatest wonder of man. Yes, it can play tricks on us, and its awesome capacities do not, unfortunately, prevent all of us from being enormously stupid at times; fundamentally, however, it is your greatest asset and one you can easily and quickly nourish. That's why, to repeat my subtitle:

  > You are much better than you think

  and the mention of 'better' prompts the closely related point that the very fact that you're reading these words, whether you're just browsing or (I very much hope!) have bought the book, shows that:

  > You are already interested in *getting* better.

- Just because you're not tops at something doesn't mean you're no good at it at all, and it certainly doesn't mean you should give up, using your limitations as an excuse. Instead, look on them as a potential strength which you can realise if your will is strong enough.
- The *will* is indeed paramount. If that is in proper order, then what might otherwise be dutiful slog becomes transformed into productive ambition and, thereby, achievement; in some ways, therefore, it is even more important than talent or imagination.[1]
- Don't fool around; don't fool yourself. We're all very good at excuses, at pretending we're working when we're not, at blaming

other people or other things for our own flaws and screw-ups. That this is both universal and understandable makes it doubly dangerous, not less so: you really cannot afford to indulge in such buck-passing. Conversely, however . . .

- . . . Don't be too modest and don't think you're stupid because you don't know everything or indeed as much as the pupil next to you seems to. That 'seems' is crucial: as often as not it is an illusion!

- Teachers are not only found in classrooms, and learning does not only take place in lecture halls or at one's desk.

- Always exercise your own judgement. Give an especially wide berth to easy (i.e. lazy and brain-mortgaging) internet browse-and-lift options. Above all, ensure that the item you are thinking of using at least has a named author, not just a website address: the latter are likely to be inadequate or simply terrible.

- *Organisation* and *intelligence* are not synonyms. But they should and can be made so.

- 'Self-help' defines a central truth – that students, of all kinds and aims, have it in them to improve significantly in almost everything they do. That applies whether they are conceited or, much more probable, unduly modest.

Right, let's play ball.

Launch

First, nail this into your head, or at least onto your study-bedroom wall:

> Nobody can be good at everything.

In medieval and Renaissance times, and for a while beyond, the concept of the Universal Genius enjoyed a wide currency. Such men[2] were not exactly common, naturally, but there were those who really did excel at every discipline and who produced work of the highest distinction: one thinks of Michelangelo, Leonardo da Vinci, arguably Shakespeare (a much undersung naturalist who also thoroughly understood contemporary science and cosmology), Milton and – probably the last such figure – Goethe (1749–1832). Shortly after him, the phenomenon withered into extinction, and it is relevant to the ambit and purposes of this book to consider briefly why that happened.

Almost all students know something about the French Revolution which began in 1789, and most have some knowledge of the American Revolution/War of Independence which came to an end six years before. Equally important in its different way was the Industrial Revolution in Britain, which was spawned at around the same time. But arguably the most important revolution of all was a far less violent or even visible one: the revolution in *knowledge*.

Our own time has become virtually synonymous with 'the information explosion', and given the internet, the near-miraculous search engines which serve and nourish it, and the seismic advances in computing technology and the like, it is not surprising that the concept is on most people's minds and lips. We shall consider the phenomenon in proper detail in subsequent chapters and also Appendix I; for now all I'd like to point out is that:

> information is not *at all* the same thing as knowledge

and, moreover, that the primary aim of every successful student should be to convert *mere information* into *genuine knowledge* that s/he possesses and can apply with confident mastery.

The knowledge revolution that characterised the early nineteenth century was engendered by a colossal spurt of discoveries in almost every field of human learning. Of course, technology was one such, and it advanced apace along with everything else; however, we're talking here about the invention of new machinery, gadgetry and the foundation of all that we now take for granted about national infrastructures, not on the dazzling appliance of IT, whose chief property and value is *speed*.

One consequence of this exponential growth in what human beings knew about the world they lived in, how it worked and what could be done on, and mined from, it was that there was suddenly *just too much to know* to absorb it all; hence the inevitable demise of the Universal Genius. There were other, rather less rarefied consequences too. Up till then, 'Science' was a synonym for 'knowledge' – unsurprisingly, since the former derives from the Latin *scio*, meaning 'I know'.[3] Almost equally suddenly, 'Science' came to denote specific disciplines – Biology, Chemistry, Physics, Geology, Pathology and Medicine; later would come many more denominations, including Psychology and Psychiatry. Thus was born the division of knowledge into Science and Arts/Humanities.[4]

In some ways, I suppose, this was an inevitable process. However, I am far from alone in considering it a most regrettable one. In 1962 the novelist and distinguished scientist C.P. Snow famously launched the 'Two Cultures' debate; his thesis – which at root contended that in all too many instances the Sciences and the Arts had become separate territories which regard each other with mystification, even hostility – is still uncomfortably apposite. That kind of intellectual apartheid encourages a 'box mentality' which can even infect students who are doing only Humanities subjects. They don't do it on principle or purpose, naturally, but they do tend to put (say) History, French and English into 'boxes', and can be disconcerted if their English teacher makes any significant reference to matters historical or to a French text, or if their History teacher starts talking about the literature of the 1920s as a revealing index of what was happening during that decade.

Schools themselves are hardly blameless in this, though it would not be fair to be too censorious. First, they are subject to law, government policy, the specifications (= 'orders') of the Qualifications and Curriculum Authority, and thereby to such dubious phenomena as league tables and Ofsted monitoring – all of which means they have less academic liberty and independence[5] than they would like or, indeed, should have. Second, they are trapped in a situation of their own making, at once paradoxical and apparently irresoluble. One might be deeply sympathetic about that entrapment, but that doesn't make it any less serious or problematic. And because it can especially affect the kind of student whom this book is addressing, it needs exploring.

I have yet to see a school prospectus that does not centre on the given institution's wide-ranging array of opportunities, activities, facilities and areas of learning. That 'pitch' hinges on the idea – or rather *ideal* – of the 'all-rounder'. Now it goes without saying that everyone – parents, teachers, students themselves – wants our young people to receive as enrichingly broad an education as possible. We all want the young adults who leave school for university or employment to be academically competent or better; to be aesthetically literate – music, theatre, art; to be healthy and fit, and (where appropriate) trained athletes; to be versed in matters of citizenship, including racial awareness, financial management, spiritual and moral awareness . . . and so on. The list is not quite endless, but it is pretty prodigious, and the range of things that many schools do genuinely provide (as opposed to claiming to do so in those glossy prospectuses!) is highly impressive.

The paradox – and trouble – comes in the form of the curriculum itself. It is all very well to talk of the 'all-rounder', but the term soon seems glib when one takes a good look at what happens from Year 10 (fourteen years old) in the UK and a number of other countries too. That's when specialisation sets in. Oh yes, all students have to do the

Core subjects (English, Maths and Science); they must also do at least one foreign language and one Humanity. But even at this middle school stage it is quite easy for pupils to 'weight' their choices in one direction or another. Those who see themselves (or are encouraged to do so by others) as scientists can opt for Design and Technology and choose Geography as their Humanity, which is a highly debatable identification.[6] Conversely, the Arts-oriented student can get away with following an all-Humanities course, with the exception of compulsory Double Award Science.

Of course, many other students *do* follow a more balanced curriculum in Years 10 and 11. But two points need to be made. The first is as embarrassing as it is by now obvious: no student is *required* to pursue such a balanced choice, and that immediately renders the conceit that we are a nation of academic all-rounders a mendacious fiction.[7] The second is because most pupils know that their academic horizons will shrink when they reach fourteen, the rot can set in considerably earlier than that. They become acclimatised, even conditioned, to viewing certain subjects with indifference or dislike; they don't bother because they know that soon those subjects won't matter: in a real sense, they won't exist. Okay, the intervening years will consequently involve a good deal of boredom in the lessons in question; however, pupils are pretty good at dealing with boredom anyway, and they intuitively know that there's not much anyone can do about it. As Dr Johnson wisely observed:

Men may be persuaded, but not pleased, against their will.

As I trust has been evident from my first sentence, I am entirely sympathetic to young people who suffer from 'learning blocks', who find they struggle to enjoy and therefore cope with certain subjects or specific areas of those subjects, or who, for one reason or another, feel inferior to their classmates in this facility or that. But it also saddens me – mainly because it doesn't have to be like that: to use the term in its full philosophical sense, it is not *necessary*. That's why I've written this book, and to take that declaration further, here are some important reflections by a colleague of mine – Ian Sheldon, Head of Chemistry at my school. I shall be quoting the whole letter in the next chapter, but for now these points are as salient as they might be surprising:

'Chemistry is hard.' If you polled a representative cross section of schoolchildren past and present, that would be the consensus.

I base that judgment on two things. First, if I had a fiver for every parent who has said to me during a parents' evening, 'Of course, I was never any good at Chemistry,' or 'Well, I'm no help to him, I gave up the subject as soon as possible,' I would be considerably richer than I am now. It's almost as if they are *proud* not to have the slightest clue what I'm trying to teach their sons . . . I wonder whether this happens in other subjects? Do people freely admit to their inadequacies in English, for example?

. . . Chemistry is *not* hard. Whenever I say that to a set, they say, 'You would say that, you understand it.' True, I do understand school Chemistry, and therefore I do find it easy. True, as Chris Tarrant would say, 'It's only easy when you know the answer.' But the subject itself is no more difficult than any other. Certainly up to [Year 12] it's pretty black and white – you either know it or you don't. There's nowhere to hide. Get out and learn the facts!

Tough stuff. But absolutely right – and in two ways. First, it exposes the quasi-genetic excuse that, as Ian suggests, is all too common – and to answer the two questions at the end of his first paragraph, 'Yes, it does, and yes, they do.' Not too long ago a German teacher told me that a parent had said to her, 'I can't get all that worked up about his lack of progress in the subject. After all, we won the war, didn't we?' – a combination of non-logic and parental dereliction that takes some beating. The English equivalent I encounter most often is, 'I've never liked Shakespeare, so you can't really expect him to, can you?'. Just like Ian's theoretical fiver-earners, that is not just a river of drivel: it is both insulting to the teacher concerned and, more important, a subtle but pernicious form of parental delinquency. If you load the guns before your son or daughter even goes into the classroom, you shouldn't be surprised if they shoot themselves in the foot.

Second, Ian's analysis draws unanswerable attention to the fact that:

Learning is as much the student's responsibility as the teacher's.

You might find that observation not only stern but somewhat bewildering, given the oceanic number of hand-outs you doubtless receive in many, perhaps all, of your classes. (How on earth did the teaching profession cope prior to the invention of the photocopier?) In an age obsessed by qualifications, grade-percentages, 'standards' and all manner of 'accountability' issues, teachers are under almost as much 'outcome pressure' as the students themselves; have you noticed how nervous your teachers are on Results Day?! It therefore figures that teachers of all kinds and in all disciplines find themselves, against all their deepest inclinations, not only spoon-feeding their charges but occasionally *force-*feeding them.

That might be understandable, but it is deeply deplorable. It is the antithesis of the 'independent learning' that so many schools, think-tanks and quangos *talk* of sponsoring; it indicates a culture based on fear, not on enablement. And it insidiously encourages many students to regard themselves as sponges, especially in those subjects they don't like much or in which they are not 'naturals'. That is wrong, and in the most basic way possible: the word 'education' comes from the Latin *educo*, meaning 'to draw out': it does *not* mean 'to pour in'.

Where does that leave you, and how can I help? Well, all I've been saying in these initial pages hinges on three things potentially injurious to all students but perhaps especially so to those who are not 'naturals' in this subject or that:

Barriers   Bigotry   Band-wagons

I happen to be a passionate jazz enthusiast, and one of my favourite musicians is the tenor saxophonist Sonny Rollins. He once observed: 'A lot of times, jazz means no barriers.' He was talking about racial and social freedoms, but his remark not only can be applied to the listening experience itself: by extension it touches on one of my fundamental purposes in this book.

Academic *barriers* have been with us ever since 'Science' came to mean something other than 'Knowledge'. And while it would be farci-cally self-deluded to imagine I can overturn two hundred years of History with a single, slimmish volume, the primary aim of *Passing Your Weak Subjects* is to persuade you that it is possible to prosper at them almost or just as much as in the areas where you are naturally strong.

Don't think of your subjects as separate, law-unto-themselves species; don't 'box' things in such a way. It is psychologically false – people do not naturally think in compartments (or if they do they're not very good thinkers) – and it is academically disabling. From Chemistry to Theology, from English to Physics, from French to Applied Mathematics, all subjects require (and will reward) the same ability to focus, to master ongoing detail in a systematic way, and to be *in charge* of what you're doing. Yes, some of those details will come more easily to you than others, but you'll get there in all areas if you approach your studies in a consistent way.

That is why the heart of this book – both geographically and academically – is Chapter 3, 'Making it stick: top tips by subject'. If you care to glance through it now, or soon, you will quickly see that some eighty per cent of what each subject expert advises is common to *all* the disciplines covered; sometimes the very phrasing is nearly identical. And that is no sterile exercise in multiple duplication: on the contrary, it is heavyweight proof and endorsement of the principle that if you get your attitudes right, build sound techniques and working habits, and engage with the material at issue rather than try passively to absorb it or just turn away from it, you can be as successful as the apparent 'born high-fliers' that you may have in your class. It is possible that such students may be naturally more gifted than you in some areas, but at least part of their strength is knowing how to apply those gifts, strengthen and broaden them. You can do that too.

The *bigotry* I have in mind might be less obviously offensive than its racist and sexist incarnations, but it can still harm you badly. It is not, I freely admit, easy to do this, but if anyone in your family has an obvious prejudice against this or that area of the curriculum, try to ignore them politely, or anyway privately decide not to follow that route yourself. It is always a tough, almost 'watershed' moment for young people when they realise that their parents are not always right; it is even tougher when they're forced to recognise that the advice or judgments they're being fed are just silly, or worse.[8] But such recognition is essential if you are to flourish. The same goes for any similar prejudices voiced by your contemporaries, particularly if they are your friends. Don't fall out with them, but pay no heed either.

Finally, my citing of *band-wagons* signifies the pressures and aggressive momentum engendered by government targets, the (ludicrous) belief that 'results' are synonymous with 'standards', the obsession with product as opposed to process, and the consequent effect on how lessons get taught. They are *big* band-wagons – indeed juggernauts – and, as will be evident, I consider their effect to be largely other than affirmative or enabling. But they can be side-stepped: they do not have to turn you into a dutiful or bored sponge. Look to learn from your teachers in every way you can; look to find ways of making the subject matter to you. If all else fails, remember this:

> An enormous number of achievements – small, medium and large
> – are fuelled by a mixture of vanity and rage.

Show yourself, and others, how good you can be; show those who enragingly doubt you (including, perhaps, you yourself) just how wrong they are. To do so is immensely satisfying, and creates confidence and energy for future success too.

To close this chapter, it is not only worth your reflecting anew on my 'mantra':

> you are better than you think

but also on the fact that

> you are immensely lucky.

The last thing I want to do is come on like some faded preacher, but please take a good look at the extract below.

Global Village: A Weekly Posting from Cyberspace

The Times Magazine, Saturday 10 May, 2003

You should be so lucky

If we could shrink the earth's population to a village of precisely 100 people, with all the existing human ratios remaining the same, there would be:

57	Asians
21	Europeans
14	from the Western hemisphere, both north and south
8	Africans
52	would be female
48	would be male
70	would be non-white
30	would be white
70	would be non-Christian
30	would be Christian
89	would be heterosexual
11	would be homosexual
6	people would possess 59 percent of the world's wealth – and all 6 would be from the United States
80	would live in sub-standard housing

70	would be unable to read
50	would suffer from malnutrition
1	would be near death
1	would be near birth
1	(yes, just 1) would have a college education
1	would own a computer

If you have food in the fridge, clothes on your back, a roof overhead and a place to sleep, you are richer than 75% of this world. If you have money in the bank and spare change somewhere, you are among the top 8% of the world's wealthy. And if you can read this message, you are more blessed than more than the two billion people in the world who cannot read at all.

I hope you find all that information as uneasily fascinating as I do. It spells out more devastatingly than any single piece I have read just how fortunate I am to have been able (among much else) to write this book and, likewise, how fortunate you are to be able to read it in the comfort of your own well-appointed home, complete with PC and all other domestic facilities. (That's still true even if you find the book worthless!)

I want to help you use that luck and that giant brain of yours. On now to how to get the latter into proper working shape.

Chapter 2

Sorting it
Getting the mind-set right

The fault . . . is not in our stars, but in ourselves.

Julius Caesar

You must be *in charge*

Not just students but people in all walks of life and at all ages do certain things less successfully than they might because, for a variety of reasons, they think they *can't* do them, or do them very well. This belief has a number of sources and assumes a number of consequent forms. All ten statements that follow I have heard (and occasionally said!) at some time, but they are exemplary rather than exhaustive: you could probably nominate a further ten in very little time.

1 My star sign is Pisces, and Pisceans aren't fitted for that sort of work.
2 I'm spiritual/artistic, not practical.
3 What's the point of learning to cook? There are restaurants, aren't there? And there are more convenience-food packages available than anyone could get through in a lifetime.
4 I'm good at anything linear (languages, algebra) but I'm poor at anything visual or spatial.
5 Why learn to swim? The chances of drowning are less than those of being hit by lightning, especially if you stay away from water more than two feet deep.
6 It's not worth bothering with this in the first place – dull, joyless and ultimately futile.
7 My teacher is awful – unsympathetic and unable to communicate.
8 For me, learning has to be *fun*. Chemistry/Geography/whatever don't begin to qualify.

9 What's the point in learning to drive? Haven't you heard of taxis?
10 Sorry, it just doesn't suit me. I can't help it.

Some of those are plausible, others highly doubtful, and one or two just silly. All of them, however, are *excuses* rather than *reasons*. And:

> No student who's looking for success, be that on a limited or spectacular scale, can afford to *pretend* – which is what excuses invariably involve.

Nor are excuses the only form of pretence. Just as harmful are the false crutches that many students adopt, thinking they will heal all disabilities and foster lasting health. They do no such thing: anything that causes you to surrender responsibility and control to something other than your own brain and self is *crippling*, not enabling.

Why real achievers don't do drugs

The drugs in question are nothing to do with those that are smoked, sniffed, swallowed or syringed. I have in mind a quite different kind of 'Class A Substance Abuse'; curiously enough, they too all begin with 'S':

- self-delusion;
- superstition;
- smart-alec ruses;
- stealing;
- study aids and surfing the net;
- spell-check.

The last two are fairly recent comers to the party; the others have been around almost as long as humankind itself. All six can seriously damage a student's health, if not indeed ruin it.

- If you imagine that your chances of succeeding in an exam hinge on whether or not you 'have a good day' or on whom your examiner might be, you are being both *self-deluded* and *superstitious* and that will cost you dearly unless you change your thinking.
- If you think that impressing a marker or an examiner is a matter of flashy presentation or clever-clever 'performance art', you are again deluding yourself and also adopting a *smart-alec* attitude; that too will cost you dearly.

- And if you believe that *study aids* and *surfing the net* will guarantee you high success, you are playing an extremely dangerous game that might result in losing everything you're going for. First, you are substituting secondary sources for irreplaceable primary ones – your syllabuses, your texts, your teachers and above all your own brain. Second, a great number of such aids, either in pulped-tree or electronic form, are mediocre; many are distinctly poor; some are almost indescribably bad.

Those six 'drugs' are bad news in and of themselves. Moreover, just as much as physical narcotics, they erode, often rapidly, your most priceless asset:

You.

As already telegraphed, the mantra 'I am in charge' should be adopted by all students, whether they are gifted or think of themselves as ordinary. If you think exams are a lottery and examiners stupid, gullible or hostile, *you are not in charge*. If you think snazzy fonts, beautifully manicured handwriting and other forms of surface charm are more important than substance, *you are not in charge*. If you mortgage your brain to the whims of this study aid hack or that internet clown, *you are not in charge*. With that imperative in mind, let's look at each of those 'S' words in detail.

Self-delusion

I've already dealt with self-delusion via that opening litany of excuses, and it is revisited in the next section too. All I want to add now is that, in a way, it is additionally an umbrella term that covers the other five, and that once you become clear-sighted about what you are and what you have and what you truly need to do, self-delusion will not be a problem, and that, as a result, although the other five will still need to be resisted, they will be less likely to corrupt you.

Superstition

We are all, to some degree, prone to superstition. Rare if not unique is the person who has not spoken of 'fingers crossed' or 'touching wood', declared 'third time lucky' or cited 'Friday the thirteenth' as a reason for things having gone badly. That may be harmless gibberish, but gibberish it is; and it becomes anything *but* harmless when otherwise sentient people organise their lives according to whether Uranus is in the House of Saturn or any and all other astrological nonsense.

I'm not indulging in scabrous prejudice but making a point fundamental to the fortunes of all ambitious people, students or otherwise. The capacity to succeed lies primarily in *you*. Other factors, such as the quality of your teachers and fellow students, the resources at your disposal, even the occasional stroke of luck, might play their part, but you are, by a mile, the main actor.

> If things go well, that is to your credit; if things do not, that is your fault.

That's a summary as tough as it is bald, and on occasion it won't be quite fair – either way. But I am convinced it is largely true.

Superstition covers a multitude of sins – and that's *exactly* what they are for any ambitious student. Even if you despise astrological explanations as much I do, you may still believe it's a matter of sheer chance whether you'll get a fair examiner or a nasty one, whether the question will be to your taste or impossible to do, and – most of all – whether you'll have one of your good days or the reverse. All that is silly, self-wounding mumbo-jumbo – the kind of sub-thinking that jettisons everything that makes you *in charge*. Becoming a successful student owes nothing to chance; it is a matter of applied reasoning, logic and organisation.

Smart-alec ruses

Nobody likes smart-alecs; nobody respects them either. The smart-alec is the wise guy who fools only himself, the posturer who is all veneered style and no substance, the know-it-all whose lordly cynicism is that of the unworldly and the inadequate.

That's a very stern summary, and in truth I've encountered very few students in thirty years who have been that disagreeable! But even when not without charm, the smart-alec is someone who believes getting ahead, or even just getting by, hinges on 'putting one over' on somebody or something. Here is a selection of smart-alec sallies with which teachers are all too familiar:

1   Sorry about your essay assignment: I forgot.
2   Sorry about your assignment: the printer crashed.

3 Sorry I haven't completed your homework: illness in the family.
4 Sorry I missed your lesson: I just lost all track of what time it was.

Number 1 is the worst, as well as the most frequent. Whether the perpetrator realises it or not, it de-codes as 'I couldn't be bothered to remember', and is never anything other than deeply unimpressive. The other three invariably fall on the ear as tired (and tiresome) excuses – even when they are perfectly genuine, which of course can apply at times. But they still fall under the 'smart-alec' banner for a separate and even more fundamental reason:

> In all four, the use of 'your' is deluded and a dereliction: implicitly if not explicitly, it dramatises the assumption that a student's work is the teacher's responsibility.

That is not so. The teacher's responsibility is to enable learning in every way that s/he can – through class teaching, naturally; structured programmes of work; detailed and illuminating marking; much else. Doing the resultant work is the student's task, no one else's. I am very fortunate in the students I currently teach, and rare are the occasions when I come up against recidivist late-submitters (and it's no accident that the above four sallies and their variants tend to be trotted out by the same students). When I do, I eventually find myself saying:

> 'Look, when are you going to understand that I get paid whether you do the work or not? It's *your* essay, not *mine*.'

Until students realise that it is their work, not the teacher's, they will regard almost all assignments as a chore that they must complete out of duty, not desire or pleasure. That is not a recipe for any kind of success, which needs grown-up commitment, not smart-alec side-stepping.

You might find some of those recent remarks unfriendly, even rather pompous; so be it, though I hope it's not the case. But any waspishness or severity is founded on a conviction that many more students under-achieve through over-dependence on alibis and ruses than through lack of talent, and also that any such feinting is, in its way, as dishonest as the next 'S'.

Stealing

I'm not talking about the odd occasion when you reproduce someone else's answer during a test, or desperately borrow your friend's Maths homework first thing in the morning and submit the copied work as your own. We've all done that, and while it's hardly admirable, nobody sane is going to get all that steamed about such sporadic offences. The kind of robbery I have in mind is called *plagiarism*, and it can cost the student more dearly than any other of the vices and traps we're investigating.

Whatever its particular incarnation, plagiarism is nothing more nor less than intellectual theft; nevertheless, there are, I think, two kinds of plagiarist:

> the 'cynical' and the 'innocent'.

The former culprits are either too lazy or too diffident (possibly both) to do any work themselves, simply ripping off whole swathes of others' efforts. That is not only extremely shabby: *it is very stupid.*

All writers have an individual voice, a perceptible stylistic signature. In the case of the beginner this may be halting and as yet raw, but it's still there, and anyone familiar with your work will recognise it. If you suddenly ape the style – and thinking – of an international authority, or even an internet chancer whose stuff has mistakenly impressed you, it won't take a forensic scientist to spot what you've done.

'Innocent' plagiarism may be less morally disreputable but it's just as damaging. This comes about through a different kind of laziness born of bad organisation and resulting in last-minute panic: yes, you meant to acknowledge this source and that quotation, but you were past your assignment deadline and you didn't have time. There is only one answer to that – well, only one they'll let me print – and it is:

> Rubbish!

Another 'smart-alec alibi' which is fully as convincing as a 'photograph' of the Loch Ness Monster. Footnotes, acknowledgements and a bibliography are as much a part of your assignment as its title and the main text itself. In addition, even if your marker believes your feeble sob-story, you're still going to be down-graded for the fault.

My last point about plagiarism is introduced by the words of a friend and highly experienced colleague:

> 'By now it is much easier for pupils to nick things than it is for us to determine where or from whom it was nicked.'

Partly because they have grown up with the net rather than adapted to it in middle age (never easy!), teenage students are much more proficient at 'lifting' material than are teachers, markers and examiners at establishing its provenance. There *are* some effective police forces around – notably the website www.turnitin.com, used by many IB (International Baccalaureate) schools, all universities in the UK and a vast number of American colleges and universities worldwide. But in truth, the cops are never going to catch up with the robbers here; for a start, they're outnumbered.

That is not offering you a licence to steal! Quite the reverse: what I've just been discussing is the most dangerous snare of all. It may be true that the cops will never catch *all* the robbers, but they will catch *some*. You don't want to be in that number, do you? Being caught out, whatever you've done, is always humiliating, but that's not the worst thing that might happen if you plagiarise. You could have your work disqualified – and not just in the perpetrated subject but right across the board. This really is a case where honesty is the best policy. It's also the simplest one, allowing you to get on with showing how good you are, guilt-free and fully focused.

Now to the last two 'S Words'.

Study aids and surfing the net

First of all, let's establish precisely what I mean by 'study aids', starting with what I *don't* mean. I am *not* talking about:

- decent text books;
- scholarly works with an evident and distinguished pedigree;
- standard and specialist reference books;
- material issued by your teachers;
- guides such as this one!

The first is essential and all the others highly desirable. No, the scorn that you doubtless noted in this chapter's opening remarks is directed at those commercially produced 'Pass Notes' and the like which either duplicate what your texts, teachers and you are doing anyway or – worse and more often – subvert and contaminate all that by being badly written, wrong-headed or just plain wrong. And I'm tempted to add just the curt injunction

stay well away from them

and move swiftly on.

However, that would be too simple and therefore of very limited assistance to you. Besides, there are two quite distinct considerations at issue:

- quality, and
- user-psychology

– and they warrant separate scrutiny.

Concerning the first, I might have overstated the case, or else the state-of-play is more cheering in other subjects than in my own main one, English. Certainly, several valued colleagues mention with approval certain study aids in their 'top tips' in Chapter 3. I bow to their particular wisdom, and I'm sure you can trust what they recommend. But if you contemplate purchasing others, I urge you to exercise caution and as much judgement as you can muster. There are some enabling publications of this type around, yes, but a great many are lifelessly mediocre and more than a few are frankly terrible. And without being condescending, a student is very unlikely to *know* which is which, at least in the initial minutes prior to buying or not buying. One only acquires that kind of acumen when one's knowledge of the topic or area in question is tolerably comprehensive – and it could easily be argued that by such a stage, you don't need the study aid anyway!

Let me resignedly assume, though, that you've overridden my advice and bought one or more of the pesky things. Let me further assume that either by luck or judgement, you've chosen well. The situation is still precarious, indeed potentially injurious – which is where your *user-psychology* comes in.

Even a really good study aid – well-written, entertaining, illuminating – quickly becomes a very bad one if you allow it to control your subsequent work. If you come to know the study aid better than the text it annotates, you have surrendered control. If you've memorised techniques it recommends for remembering information but cannot yet remember the actual information in question, you have surrendered control. Above all, you have surrendered control if the study aid has come to supersede what is on offer in class and your response to it. In the end, academic success at any stage and at all levels of achievement hinges on

a healthy partnership between your brain and your teachers'.

If you get that right, study aids will at most be an occasionally useful, minor back-up; the rest of the time, they will be a needless expense and an irrelevant mirage. You wouldn't buy a road atlas and expect it to teach you how to drive, would you? Save yourself a lot of time, boredom and money.

In turning our attention to *surfing the net*, I am aware that it is almost certainly a dated phrase now, and I apologise for my un-hip slang. But the term remains useful for my purposes here, suggesting as it does a skimming, largely ludic (i.e. playful) activity. Now, there's absolutely nothing wrong with *play* as such: I'll be showing that it can assume a decisive role when studying. But you cannot afford to *confuse* work and play, to pretend you're doing real research when all you're doing is the website equivalent of TV channel-hopping. Because it's still relatively new and exciting, and also sexily fashionable, the net can be dangerously seductive, conning you into three hours' browsing that is a waste of your time even if you download a lot of 'interesting-looking' material.

It is dangerously seductive in two other ways as well. The first is its awesome size. It's not just that virtually every commercial, academic and political organisation on the planet has its own website; there are by now tens of millions of individuals who can say the same. And in truth its democratic nature is one of the net's great virtues: anyone can publish on it. But it only takes a moment or two's thought, I trust, to see that this is also one of its vices, or at any rate a huge potential snare. Just because it's there doesn't mean it's reliable. Consequently, and closely akin to those times when you consider buying a study aid:

You need to exercise great care and even greater *judgment*.

Consulting the net is a beguiling, even semi-mesmerising activity, and I would press you to increase your level of concentration and scepticism: don't let the magic get to you! Ask yourself:

- Is this really any good?
- Can I check it out independently/confirm its reliability elsewhere?
- Is it truly relevant to what I'm doing? Does it add weight and authority to my own work?

If all the answers are affirmatives, great. But one last question remains, and it's the most important:

Is it *better* than anything I could do?

I am not encouraging conceit in you, but you have plenty of talent and you shouldn't be shy about it. If the item you've unearthed really is strengthening, then by all means use it; however, I think you'll find that as often as not you'll do just as well on your own. And, needless, to say, *don't steal!*

Spell-check

By the end of this book I may have driven you half-crazy with my fulminations on this matter, but that's a chance I'm prepared to take if it immunises you against the septic practices so many students follow.

In her admirable *Notepad to Mousepad* Judith Woolf advises students to:

> learn to use a spell-check. *Learn* is the operative word here . . .

The italics are mine, not the author's: evidently, I consider the point even more important than she does! If you don't do as she says, spell-check will become another destructive drug, not an aid. Your brain must stay in charge, for I'm afraid that:

> Computers don't do context.

Only human brains can do that. Remember, too, that it is human brains that concocted the spell-check software in the first place, and that on the evidence I've seen, some of those brains are rather less reliable and informed than they should be or than yours is likely to be.

The two sections above have concentrated on what not to do, what to avoid, what to banish. That was quite deliberate, if apparently negative: success often starts with understanding why certain things are wrong and seeing why and how they don't work. It is now time, though, to look at how to get things right.

The absolute need for clarity

A great deal of what even the brightest and most articulate people say and write is *not clear*: it is prone to misinterpretation, either accidental or wilful, and especially if the language is English (the richest and most complex of all the world's tongues), the chances of ambiguity are constant and high.

So, to launch this section, I want to look at the way people say or write things that they might think are clear but which aren't. Some of them are funny, even silly; one or two are very much otherwise. But all of them matter. And if this general principle seems somewhat high-flown, it is still one worth pursuing:

> Your aim as a speaker or writer: *never* to be in a position where you need to say, 'That's not what I meant, at all.'[1]

And although I shall be largely concentrating on the written word as opposed to other symbologies that attend Maths, the sciences, Geography and so on, all my observations can be applied to all subjects. Be quite sure you've logged what you want to say and only what you want to say, and the results should be trouble-free.

Possibly the most common form of ambiguity is *syntactical ambiguity* – that is, a flaw in word order.

- For sale: grand piano owned by a lady with ornately carved legs.
- 33-year-old Mrs Jones admitted to dangerous driving in Leeds Crown Court yesterday.

Simple – and, I hope, amusing – enough. But these two are more subtle, though equally flawed:

1 The record was out of stock, which John wanted.
2 The government will announce that the electricity supply is to be cut off tomorrow.

In (1) it is not clear whether the record John wanted was out of stock or whether he *wanted it to be* out of stock; maybe it was a dire CD his sister had told him to buy and whose sounds he dreaded hearing on his return home!

In (2) it is unclear whether it is the government's *announcement* that will take place tomorrow or its *action*. To those who argue that the second is so unlikely in its summary no-notice severity as to render the charge of ambiguity irrelevant, all I can say without being unduly cynical is that governments are capable of anything, especially in extreme circumstances.

This next is almost impenetrably ambiguous, in that it admits of two radically different tones and therefore meanings:

> We should not tolerate those homeless people living in our streets.

It can signify either an absolute intolerance of homeless people themselves or an impassioned belief that society should do something about the situation and house those homeless people. A huge difference – yet unless the speaker's face is visible and voice audible (which does not apply to the written word, obviously), it is impossible to say which was the 'intended' meaning.

Ambiguity can also mean or involve vagueness. There follow eleven definitions of the word 'liberal':[2]

1 belief in a permissive society;
2 belief in freedom of speech, of association, of choice;
3 belief that certain restrictive laws should be relaxed;
4 belief that the state should interfere as little as possible in citizens' lives;
5 belief in laissez-faire economic policies;
6 supports the liberal democratic party;
7 not strict;
8 politically left-wing;
9 wishy-washy;
10 generous;
11 soft on crime.

Problematic in the extreme. A person could embody many of these beliefs and characteristics and not be a liberal; conversely, one might be a liberal and not have several of them.

The only recourse is to 'define one's terms', as early as possible. That might seem, and sometimes *is*, tedious; however, unless one does so, the chances of meaningless and fruitless discussion/argument are very high. That unfortunate outcome is even more likely when the term in question is a *loaded* one, or has become so out of secondary considerations.

A huge number of words – probably most of them – have both a *denotative* meaning and a *connotative* one. The former adjective derives from the verb *denote*: put simply, it signifies the *dictionary definition* of the word. *Connotation* signifies overtones, resonances, implications. All of us have words that are 'special', which carry an additional private meaning, but the phenomenon applies in myriad instances to 'public' language too.

Sometimes a word's connotations can entirely replace its denotation. For the time being one simply cannot use 'gay' in its original sense of 'jolly/lively/brightly coloured': it means 'homosexual', and that's that. In the same way, 'Hiroshima' will never merely signify a Japanese city, and it will take a long time before 'September 11' is just an item on a calendar between the 10th and the 12th.

So to return to *loaded* or multiply resonant terms, the word 'feminist' is difficult. A friend who teaches CT asked his students (a mixed class) what it conveyed to them, and eleven responses ensued:

Man-hating	Fighter
Lesbian	Staunch
Dungarees	Left-wing
Unshaven	Pro-abortion
Strong	Pro-women
Political	

It is very difficult there to distinguish what might be denotative ideas from connotative ones (including rank prejudice, of course). I haven't got any answers; all I want to emphasise is that awareness of the questions or the complexities will, itself, assist you in making your own thinking clearer, and assessing whether what you read or hear is sound or otherwise.

Those last two items addressed a serious and important matter. This next is neither serious nor important – except that in its very ludicrousness it does establish a basic principle.

What is wrong here? In how many ways could these instructions be misunderstood? Be as picky and exhaustive as you can, including the listing of any important *omissions*.

Instructions for Driving a Car

1   Sit behind the steering wheel.
2   Adjust mirror for best rear view.
3   Ensure handbrake is on.
4   Put gear lever into neutral.
5   Turn key to right.
6   Rotate engine until it fires.
7   Depress accelerator until engine can be heard running fast.
8   Select first gear.
9   Allow clutch pedal to gently rise while depressing accelerator still further.
10   Take off handbrake.

11   Wink in the direction you are going.
12   Grip steering wheel at ten to two.
13   If you need to brake read the following instructions . . .

One can have a lot of fun with that, for either a few minutes or (as I found with a Year 9 class recently) virtually an entire lesson. But a serious point emerges out of all this criminal idiocy – that writing even the most elementary instructions is strewn with pitfalls. One could, indeed, say it is the fiercest task that can confront any writer, especially if catering for the absolute beginner, which I assume to be the case here. Your writing needs to be spotlessly clear; you cannot afford the remotest ambiguity or anything that might confuse; above all, you must take nothing for granted, nothing at all. It is an unremitting task, and it is perhaps unsurprising that so many instructions are flawed.

One more laugh, then a grim finale. Here is one of three exemplars of 'The Funniest Jokes in the World' as researched by the British Association of Science LaughLab Society (a joke in itself, you might say) and reported by Adam Sherwin in *The Times*, Monday 14 August 2006:

> Two New Jersey hunters are in the woods when one falls to the ground. He doesn't seem to be breathing and his eyes are glazed. The other calls the emergency services.
>
> He gasps: 'My friend is dead! What can I do?' The operator says: 'Just take it easy. First, let's make sure he's dead.' There is silence, then a shot is heard. The hunter's voice comes back across the line. 'OK, now what?'

My final example melds the business of writing utterly clear instructions and the need to beware of literal-minded interpretations of words or idioms. It is a tragic one, furnished by Christopher Turk and John Kirkman in their 1982 *Effective Writing*:

> An aircraft fitter was instructed, during an undercarriage overhaul, to:
>   'Check undercarriage locking pin. If bent, replace.'
> He took out the pin and examined it. It was indeed bent, so he carefully put it back into the mechanism. The aircraft subsequently crashed.

As the authors point out, the (fatal) problem here is that replace can mean *either* 'put back' *or* 'substitute with a new one'; the latter was of course what was required. The subsequent disaster wasn't the fitter's fault but that of whoever wrote the manual he was dependent upon. That may be a grim way of reminding writers of their responsibilities, but if it works, so will this section have done.

Getting the little things right

The little things, the fiddly details, the general business of dotting 'i's and crossing 't's are not exactly exciting, and can often seem pretty tedious. The temptation, therefore, is to think that they don't really matter.

They do – fundamentally.

It is my overwhelming experience, not only as a teacher but as a householder, a customer, an employee and a whole host of other 'roles', that people who can't be bothered to get the little things right invariably, or at any rate eventually, make a serious mess of the big ones. The story about the bent aircraft pin which we've just absorbed offers a horrific instance of something apparently incidental being all-informing, and if as a general rule sloppiness rarely has such seismic consequences as that, it still pays to devote precise attention to the smallest detail.

In practical study terms, that means taking proper care of:

* *The mechanics of language, whether English or foreign tongues.* Nothing undermines a piece of prose, short or extended, quite so fast as inaccurate spelling, inadequate grammar (especially misuse of tenses) and, above all, inadequate or insufficient punctuation. You can have a really interesting case to make or survey to unfold, but if the basics are not in shape, not only will that irritate and distract the reader: it will almost certainly reduce the clarity and punch of the material itself.
* *Accuracy of arithmetic and other mathematical rudiments.* Exactly the same as for language (and after all, that's exactly what Maths is in its own way). In any sophisticated exercise involving Maths – which covers economics, Geography and especially Physics – the whole thing can implode, or at least become very embarrassing, if it's based on flawed adding-up or if that shortcoming intrudes part of the way through.
* *Get your dates right.* Particularly applies to History, Classical Civilisation and Religious Studies, perhaps, but rare is the subject

where dates never feature. Students who are casual about this are seldom convincing in other ways, mainly because at a foundational level they don't quite know what they're talking about.

- *Make sure your drawings and diagrams are accurate/properly to scale.* One of the most wonderful things about perusing great artists' preliminary sketches is to realise anew how superbly well they could *draw* as well as paint. Of course, one shouldn't be surprised by that: if you're an indifferent draughtsman, you're not going to make it as a painter, whatever foolish and myopic remarks are still sometimes made about Picasso and other modernists. Now, you don't have to be a *beautiful* drawer, but you do have to be a functionally sound one: just like your Maths, your lines and angles have to add up, particularly if the diagram in question is a graph.

- *Make your research and revision 'little' and specific, not big and vague.*

Don't say	Say instead
I must work harder at my economics	I must master these two graphs and fully grasp what they mean and how they work
I must improve my punctuation	In the next half-hour I will become totally consistent in the use of quotation marks for titles; I will ensure my paragraphing is regular and consistent
I must fully understand the relationship between Oedipus and Jocasta	I shall study closely their exchanges before the mention of Laius's servant (at which 'Jocasta turns sharply') and after that
I must be sure how the human body works	By the end of this session I shall have fully absorbed the functions and behaviour of the liver and the kidneys

By now, I trust, the point has been made clearly enough. There's a proverb which runs:

Look after the pennies, and the pounds will take care of themselves.

That might not be true in the literal sense, but as a principle of good house-keeping and careful accounting it makes healthy sense. In the same way:

Look after the little things, and the big things will start falling
comfortably into place.

I have found that to be true of my own work and that of all my truly
successful students. And I've certainly found its negative converse to
be all too accurate:

Bad habits are notoriously catching.

Before moving on, a fairly extensive postscript is in order.

PS texting and emails

These still-recent innovations are here to stay, and no doubt you use
both frequently. Fine; but beware. I admit it's unlikely that the kind
of short-hand and codes that characterise many text-messages will
obtrude into your formal work, but be on your guard nonetheless. We
all use several different registers of language in any given day (of which
texting is an idiosyncratic instance), and you need to get the right one
for academic tasks.

Emailing is altogether a more insidious threat, not least because so
many adults (including, I have to say, some of my colleagues) seem to
imagine that normal standards of accuracy and indeed clarity need not
apply to emails; I am amazed by how many such writers start a letter
in lower case, think that 'i' is perfectly okay to denote the first person
singular ('I') and then punctuate on a take-it-or-leave-it basis. And that,
among other things, can send an unfortunate signal to the young.

The notion that emailing reduces the need for meticulous accuracy
is, to my mind, false, lazy and dangerous. However, it is not difficult
to see how it arose and why it has become so widespread a belief.
Newcomers and veterans alike find email a highly pressured activity.
Even when off-line and/or adding to other people's phone-bills rather
than one's own, economic considerations seem paramount, willing the
writer to get the job done as fast as possible. But in this case *speed* is
a decidedly double-edged property.

On the one hand, it is undoubtedly electronic communication's chief
virtue. It is now possible within the space of a morning for two parties
to have a multiple exchange of letters on a call-&-response basis which
explores and then settles a complicated matter – a process that might
take a week if entrusted to 'snail mail'. Moreover, with email one knows
– at once and almost invariably – whether your message has been

received: no GPO uncertainty there! And extending our attention to internet facilities, millions have found ordering goods or banking both faster and more efficient using this medium than former methods.

So far, so very good. But it is an important paradox that any virtue can become a vice; speed can become a major drawback if that property attends the email's actual composition and use of the 'Send' button. Returning to that multiple exchange outlined above:

It will be *no good at all* if each letter is not clear and accurate.

Indeed, the exchange will quickly multiply a whole lot more, in the form of irritated and tediously time-consuming enquiries:

- Why haven't you answered my chief question in email #1?
- I don't follow your paragraph #2 or #4.
- What did your last letter *mean*, please?

And of course that 'old favourite':

- You haven't attached the promised attachment.

One of the most valuable mottos in existence is the Latin *festina lente*. Its literal translation, 'hurry slowly', translates into the timelessly wise oxymoron:

More haste, less speed.

Nowhere is that 'tag' more urgently relevant than in email practice. If it is not borne in mind, such communication can turn out to be slower than its 'ordinary' alternatives and very frustrating into the bargain.

And that may be just the start of your problems. To repeat:

Bad habits are notoriously catching.

Sloppy email practice can soon spread into your more formal, considered writing. It is an insidious process, all the more dangerous for being invisible and, indeed, unconscious. Emailers who dispense with punctuation and other formal conventions will soon find themselves doing likewise in work that really does 'matter' – to *them*.

Actually, despite my inclusion of it under 'mechanical accuracy' just above, punctuation is *anything but a 'little thing'*. On the contrary, it is by some distance the most important 'basic skill' of them all.

Bad spelling and faulty grammar are of course to be avoided, but unless they are ludicrously poor, they hamper rather than cripple: the reader can still follow what's being said.

Bad punctuation *does* cripple, even destroy meaning. At best it leads to chronic ambiguity, at worst sheer senselessness. Moreover, deficient punctuation not only makes the reader's life a nightmare: it suggests a writer who isn't thinking or, perhaps, *cannot* think.

If you have already perused Chapter 3 as tentatively suggested, or when you come to do so, you will find that the first of twenty-four items I log for your implementation is 'attention to detail'. That is as it should be: that is where you should start. The 'little things' might be unglamorous, but attending to them from the outset means that you will

> build on rock, not on sand.

'It's not the teacher, it's the subject'

One hears this, either directly or in reported form, from a host of parents, some head teachers and even some assistant teachers, and what I want to say about it at once is:

> It is the biggest educational lie of all.

Of course it's the teacher. A good or great one can inspire you, take you into realms of both interest and achievement you did not think possible. Conversely, an inadequate or poor teacher can either serve you badly, abort your interest, or both. And what I particularly dislike about this pernicious drivel is that it puts unkind and unjust pressure on students, making them feel that it's mainly their fault that they're not progressing or enjoying their lessons, that their priorities and judgements are faulty, and that they should focus on the subject for its own sake and regardless.

However, all that said and passionately meant, there is another angle to this phenomenon that is very much worth your consideration.

There are a number of reasons why the teacher–pupil partnership can run into trouble or not work very well. Sometimes there is a personality clash; more often, the teacher comes over as either dull or not very good, which quickly saps your energy and confidence; or the subject is one that you have always found difficult or uncongenial, and now things seem to have got worse, because the teacher is not helping you surmount those previous 'blocks' and may even be adding to them. I am of course wholly sympathetic to such eventualities; however, quite exceptional circumstances apart:

> There is nothing you can do about it: you're stuck with him/her for the year.

No matter where the school or what kind it is, changing teachers is very difficult and very rare. Most head teachers won't even consider such pupil or parent requests, on the basis of:

> If I let you do this, the flood-gates will open: everybody will want a change here or there, and managing the school will become impossible.

They also have to protect the dignity and self-esteem of their staff; you might think certain teachers don't deserve such protection, but I'm afraid that isn't the point: to a very considerable extent, the *status quo* is always safeguarded in schools, which, no matter how radical they may be in some respects, are among the most conservative institutions you will ever encounter.

So what can you do?

> *Use* what you've got/have been 'lumbered' with.

It's a good rule in life, I have found, to assume that everyone you meet has got something to offer, something from which you can learn; that holds for teachers as for all others. It is extremely unlikely that the teacher you've got is absolute rubbish: whatever you might have heard or read in certain newspaper stories, truly incompetent teachers do not last very long. So even if you don't get on very well with whomever you've got, even if s/he is unappealing, dry and apparently not very interested in you or any other student, *get what you can*: it will be a lot better than nothing.

If you do that – it takes guts and real focused determination, but it can be done – you will, automatically if almost invisibly, start to function as an independent learner. You will find that what you are able to glean from the teacher forms at least a platform you can build on. Use your friends in the same class (who are likely to have the same view and problems) and work as a co-operative. And if you think I'm being rather romantic and making the whole business sound improbably curable (and I repeat my admission that it isn't easy), such an approach is wildly preferable to turning off and giving up. If you do *that* for a whole year, the chances of recovering in the next year – even if you then get the most inspiring and brilliant teacher – are virtually zero. It will be too late. At least my suggestion allows you to float, even if you don't get to swim all that far.

Implicit in some of what I've been saying in this section is another very dangerous and damaging phenomenon which requires a separate and fully explicit enquiry.

Flashpoint Zero: unthinking prejudice[3]

I have already, in Chapter 1, referred to observations by Ian Sheldon, Head of Chemistry at my school. I now want to quote in full the letter he wrote in response to my request for a list of 'top tips' for students. Most of what he talks about is specific to his subject, or at any rate to the Sciences as opposed to Humanities. However, not only is that division (as he deftly implies) a false, even stupid one: virtually everything he addresses is fundamental to all aspects of study and to all subjects. Please read it carefully: the effort will be well worthwhile.

> Chemistry is hard. I guess if you asked a representative tranche of the general populace this would be their conclusion. I base this on two things alone. Firstly, if I was paid by the number of parents that say to me, during a parents' evening, 'of course, I was never any good at Chemistry,' or, 'well, I'm no help to him, I gave up the subject as soon as possible,' then I would be considerably richer than I am now. It's almost as if they were proud not to have the slightest clue what I'm trying to teach their sons. I don't consider our parents to be representative of the general populace, but I wonder whether this happens in other subjects? Do people freely admit to their inadequacies in English, for example? Secondly, this perception of the subject is passed on to their sons in some subliminal manner – so the difficulty of Chemistry almost becomes a given.
>
> What I would say in defence of the public perception of science is that scientists do tend to use ridiculous language to deliver their findings. Take my own Masters thesis for example, 'Electron Spin Echo Spectroscopy in Radical Pairs'. This makes it sound like a couple of fundamentalists listening to a washing machine in a cave. Perhaps I should have called it 'How plants work' as it describes some of the processes that go on during photosynthesis, but then

it wouldn't have been precise. Being precise is what good scientists do well, regardless of how ridiculous or unfathomable it makes them sound. I guess the job of the good science teacher is to translate this language into words that are in common usage, whilst instructing students on the use of the 'proper' terms that other scientists will understand. Precision and language certainly feature in my top tips.

The crux of the matter is the perception, I think. Take an underprepared boy sitting two exams on the same day, Chemistry and, say, History. We might as well call these 'Trial Exams'. In both he needs to know facts, and in both he needs to be able to explain how they link together. Because he is underprepared, he will score very few marks on either paper. To the boy, this is cruelly exposed in Chemistry because not knowing the answer tends to mean a blank piece of paper where the answer should be, and therefore Chemistry is hard. In History, at least he can write *something*, even though what he does write is complete drivel and scores nothing. In my humble opinion, History, therefore, is more accessible (note: not easier), and the boy *thinks* that it is easier.

Chemistry is not hard. Whenever I say that to a set, they say, 'you would say that, you understand it.' True, I do understand school Chemistry, and therefore I do find it easy. True, as Chris Tarrant would say, 'it's only easy when you know the answer.' But the subject itself is no more difficult than any other. It's just you can't kid yourself and bluff for half a side in the hope that you will pick up a few marks. Certainly until GCSE, it's pretty black and white – you either know it (and therefore understand it), or you don't. There's nowhere to hide. Get out and learn the facts!

Speaking as someone who was signally poor at Chemistry, I find that a sobering analysis, and I wish someone like Ian had been around to advise me at the time. And if that forlorn reminiscence is of limited value to you, several things in his letter will prove immensely helpful if you let them be – and not just in Chemistry.

> Being precise is what good scientists do well, regardless of how ridiculous or unfathomable it makes them sound.

I am not quarrelling with Ian one iota in pointing out what he says holds true of *all* disciplines; the same goes for the observation he makes immediately afterwards:

The job of the good science teacher is to translate this language into words that are in common usage, whilst instructing students on the use of the 'proper' terms that other scientists will understand.

It is also the job of the good *student* to be both precise and clear. Chapter 4 addresses 'Learning and using technical terms', which I hope will encourage and enable you further. At this point I want simply to urge you from the outset to adopt as an across-the-subjects principle the determination to be exact. If you do that, all will follow – and the ease with which it does will surprise you.

No less illuminating is Ian's comparison between Chemistry and History, especially the distinction between 'more accessible' and 'easier'. Because History (or any Humanity subject) is vaguely familiar, whereas to some people Science seems to be a wholly alien tongue, the temptation to think it 'easier' is a beguiling one. As Ian says, that is a nonsensical delusion, and the sooner you grasp that, the happier and more successful you will be.

He also provides, in 'how they link together', a splendidly simple definition of *analysis*, which is explored towards the end of the next chapter. And his final injunction is perhaps the most important of all, not just because it addresses the basis of all learning, but because in addition its focus is on

knowledge, not 'skills'

– which is absolutely as it should and indeed *must* be.

Knowledge or information *always* precedes skill

Whatever the activity in question, you cannot acquire any kind of skill until you *know*, if only in theory, what lies at its root and how you need to go about it. As proof of that, here is a little puzzle. Try not to look at the answer before you've properly tackled the question!

BAGG = William the Conqueror
BEJC = ?

The answer is *Christopher Columbus*. Why?

On the surface, that solution hinges on a *skill* – in this case alphabetical-numerical substitution.

A	B	C	D	E	F	G	H	I	J	K	L ... & so forth
0	1	2	3	4	5	6	7	8	9	10	11

B A G G therefore decodes as 1066, a date famously associated with William the Conqueror (Battle of Hastings and all that). So, turning to the second line and applying the same principle, B E J C decodes as 1492, which date is memorialised in the nursery rhyme:

> In fourteen hundred and ninety-two
> Columbus sailed the ocean blue

and of course went on to 'discover' America, even though he thought he was charting a new route to the East Indies!

QED, then. But wait a moment. The *skill* involved in solving that puzzle entirely depends on requisite *knowledge*. If you do not associate 'William the Conqueror' with '1066', you have very little chance of decoding the first line; moreover, skilful alphabetical-numerical substitution will be of no use to you unless you know about Columbus and 1492. The puzzle might mobilise your intelligence and problem-solving skills, but without the basic information also involved, you're stranded and impotent.[4]

It can only come from within

> Much of the success literature of the past fifty years [has been] filled with social-image consciousness, techniques and quick fixes – with social band-aids and aspirin that addressed the problems and sometimes even appeared to solve them temporarily but left the underlying chronic problems untouched to fester and resurface.[5]

Those are wise words, none the less so for being rather more obviously true now than when Covey first wrote them in 1989. They appear in a chapter entitled 'Inside-Out', which is an inspired phrase: my own subtitle above the extract is a variant of it. No external force can really make you care, truly energise you, decisively mobilise your energies and talents. You can't get that from any kind of bottle, packet or package (whatever their contents), or even from a deeply sympathetic and inspirationally enabling human being. I stick by my earlier declamation, '*Of course* it's the teacher', but there's a limit to what even the finest instructor can do if the instructee isn't locked-on serious about being instructed. Relevant here are some remarks made sixty years ago by the poet Philip Larkin, when he was just nineteen years old:

> When will people learn that you can't teach children what they don't know already? Education should consist of helping a child to know its own faculty – its ability, rather. Each man (generally) has one talent. Education should help him find it – should make the child say 'of course' as it recognizes with delight what it has always potentially known.[6]

These remarkably congruent observations were offered forty years later by Canadian literary critic and guru Northrop Frye:

> The teacher, as has been recognized at least since Plato's *Meno*, is not primarily someone who knows instructing someone who does not know. He is rather someone who attempts to re-create the subject in the student's mind, and his strategy in doing this is first of all to get the student to recognize what he already potentially knows, which includes breaking up the powers of repression in his mind that keep him from knowing what he knows. That is why it is the teacher, rather than the student, who asks most of the questions.[7]

Each man's last sentence strikes me as especially telling. The teacher is there to *draw out*[8] what is latent, even actively present: s/he can do that via a variety of techniques and approaches, and the best teachers effect that in multiple fashion. But even the very best can't effect a successful 'Outside-In' process: just as you can't get blood out a stone, you can't pour anything into a vessel that has no opening.

Some of that might strike you as bossy, buck-passing, or just uncaring. I don't think it is any of those. If you are serious about 'passing your weak subjects', it means that you are, more widely and indeed admirably, serious about learning. That seriousness is something nothing or nobody else can give you. But if you've got it, or can find it, you will prosper. You will also have an increasingly good time.

I end this chapter with a wonderful remark by the nineteenth-century American essayist and sage, Henry David Thoreau.

> How can we remember our ignorance, which our growth requires, when we are using our knowledge all the time?

I've made a big thing about 'knowledge' preceding any acquisition of 'skills', and equally about how essential facts are the start of knowledge, not the end. But the best and most successful students (which includes teachers and indeed all adults still interested in adding to their experience and knowledge) are even more interested in their ignorance: what they don't know is more compelling than what they do. As it happens, that is not a bad definition of 'humility'; more pressing in your case, it is also a pretty good definition of how serious students get better, happier and succeed.

I've referred more than a few times to those 'top tips'. I'm sure you agree it is about time we had a full-on look at them. They are in several respects the 'heart' of this book, so no more delay!

Chapter 3

Making it stick
Top tips by subject

This 'core' chapter has an interesting provenance and history. In the autumn of 2006, I launched at my school a one-period-per-fortnight Key Skills course for our Year 10 pupils. My own set was quite a mixed bunch, and some of their comments about subjects they found difficult or uncongenial sowed the seeds of this book as a whole. More specifically, though, for the purposes of the course I wrote to all our Heads of Department, asking if they would kindly produce ten or so 'top tips' to strengthen pupils' performance, increase their confidence and allow them to be more in charge of their work, especially if they were at present 'blocked', disenchanted or struggling.

The response was extraordinary. I had suggested a notional submission date of one month hence; everyone replied, in full, within a week (one got back to me within one hour!). Even more gratifying, as I hope you will now find, the advice was detailed, clear, expert and user-friendly.

As I telegraphed early on, you will soon see that, for all the requisite subject-specific points and the writers' stylistic individuality, there is a remarkable amount of common ground. When I first read them all, I was not amazed by that, but I was struck by it – which is faintly embarrassing, because after so many years as a teacher, lecturer and researcher, I should not really have been *remotely* surprised. Don't be as slow as me! Peruse each one individually and carefully, and see how many 'endorsing repeats' you can find. Then check those against the 'Commentary' that follows my colleagues' work. Needless to say, I am most grateful to them all, and they are properly acknowledged in Appendix III.

Biology

1   *Read ahead, read ahead, read ahead!* A subject or topic is only really boring if the student does not understand the material being

addressed. Respiratory Biochemistry, a monster of complexity, becomes a story of delicate beauty once the student understands enough to step back and say 'so *that's* how it is!' Understanding leads to engagement and this improves your motivation.

2   Reading ahead not only affords you a chance to enjoy the subject more, but also:
   • Makes you feel intelligent – you *know* the answer, even ahead of 'really bright' students.
   • Teachers (and anyone generally) find it almost impossible to discriminate between intelligent people and well-informed people.
   • Impressed (gullible) teachers have a habit of making optimistic grade forecasts and writing glowing references for students who appear well informed.
   • Reading ahead ensures that lessons serve to reinforce earlier reading, clarify what was not understood the first time, and avoid that 'Oh my God, I don't know what he/she's talking about, so I'll glaze over for a while and hope I don't get asked anything' experience.
   • Over time, this raised performance will become the usual standard. Over time you will become better informed.

3   To read ahead:
   • use the topic guides provided on the school intranet;
   • use the specimen lessons provided on the school intranet.

4   *Use mind maps* to create a pathway that makes sense to yourself. It cuts out the need for all those tiresome linking words, leaving only key words or phrases. When checking the area later, if you can retell the story using only these key words etc., then you are making progress. Go back again, this time with a blank sheet, and try to redraw your mind map. Can't do it? Then you don't know it! Start again . . .

5   *Use diagrams*: draw them, colour them in, label them to learn and understand their structure and function. Redraw the diagram – can you do it all without looking at your original diagram? Can't do it? Then you don't know it! Start again . . .

6   *Flow diagrams*: these are essential for remembering and understanding complex pathways (chemical stories!) e.g. hormonal regulation of blood glucose. Draw them, add pictures of the affected organs, make them as visual as possible.

7   *Parents*: use them. Get them to check your order of phrases. Explain
the material to them. If you can teach them, if you can make them
understand, then you understand it.
   • Can't speak coherently about the topic and use drawings or
     writing to help you? Then you don't know it. Start again . . .
     (Actually, after a little protesting, parents often come to enjoy
     this process. One even started Spanish lessons after helping his
     lad with Spanish revision.)
   • Warning: explain to parents that this is a learning exercise. Before
     you start, tell them not to get cross when you get confused. Make
     it clear that anything you don't know you'll go away and look
     at again, and that you'll try again later if you don't get it perfect.

Chemistry

1   Work out how you learn best, then . . .
2   *Learn the facts.*
3   Be precise. If you can explain a concept fully, then do so.
4   Remember that notes given in lessons 'belong' to the teacher –
    it's only by rewriting them that you take ownership of their format
    and you start to make links between concepts.
5   *Learn technical vocabulary* as you would in a modern language –
    and use it in your answers.
6   Take pride in your presentation. Marks are awarded for tables,
    diagrams and graphs. The neater they are, the easier they are to
    use in the future.
7   Buy an H pencil, a pencil sharpener and a 30 cm ruler. These are
    all necessary to draw neat graphs and diagrams.
8   Four important points for graphs – scale, labelled axes, plotting
    points, line of best fit.
9   Remember that all numerical answers should have the correct unit.
    At A-Level, use 'SVU' – sign, value, unit.
10 Read the question twice, write the answer once, not the other way
    around.
11 Learn what the verbs in a question mean – 'state, explain, calculate,
    estimate, describe' etc.
12 Look at the number of marks allocated to each question. This is
    usually the number of points needed in your answer.
13 When drawing out structures, remember the HONC rule – hydrogen
    forms one bond, oxygen two, nitrogen three, and carbon four.

14   In calculations, write down some words to explain to the examiner what you are doing. Usually, *the method carries more marks than the answer.*

15   Spend some time learning the charges on common ions – use the position in the Periodic Table to help.

16   Remember that prep accounts for twenty-five per cent of the time studying Chemistry. Don't skimp on it.

17   Don't believe anyone when they tell you that Chemistry is difficult. They just haven't got it yet.

Classics I: Latin

Although Latin and Classical Civilisation come from the same subject family they are cousins rather than siblings. Most of what you will do in Latin involves working with the Latin language to some degree, whereas Classical Civilisation requires and involves absolutely no knowledge of Classical languages at all (unless of course you are using a technical term such as *chiasmus, hendiadys, hamartia* or *hubris*). Which brings me to my first top tip:

1   *Don't use obscure technical terms unless you are absolutely sure what they mean.* If you *must* use a technical term, *please* provide a brief definition so that you show the examiner that you understand the term. There's nothing worse for an examiner than seeing a sentence like '*Antigone* is a very powerful play because of the *antithesis* between Creon's *hamartia* and Antigone's *hubris*. This causes the reader to feel *pathos.*' I exaggerate, but that sentence shows precisely no understanding of the play and its themes. Far better to stick to plain English.

2   *Don't read Latin as though it were English.* In English, word-order is of vital importance to convey meaning; in Latin *word order is largely irrelevant*; it's the *ending* that tells you where and how concepts fit into the sentence. So you need to read Latin sentences in their entirety before you even begin to try to translate them – the key idea of the sentence might be at the very end (and often is). If you try to translate 'from left to right' in the English fashion you will either:

•   turn the sentence completely back to front, or
•   sound like an alien.

3   *Concentrate on nouns and verbs.* That may indicate a very traditional approach, but I always think that the absolute key to understanding a

Latin sentence is to *find the subject and find the main verb*. If you know, for example, that 'Caesar ordered . . .' is the main idea, then you are half-way to understanding the sentence – everything else tends to snap into place: you can then ask sensible questions like 'To whom did Caesar give this order?', 'What was the order?', 'Are we told any other details such as when, or how this order was given?' and so forth.

Very often the subject will be hiding in the verb – if there's no nominative case noun nearby then the subject will be 'he', 'they', 'I' or whatever.

4 *The language is simpler than you think.* Verbs, for example, can be split into the *stem* (which gives you the basic meaning of the verb) and *ending* (which tells you the *person* and the *tense*. Learn the Latin signposts which tell you the verb tenses (e.g. stem + BA + ending = imperfect tense). Even better, verb endings actually boil down to three sets of endings:

	Active	Perfect tense active	Passive
I	-m or -o	-i	-r
You (singular)	-s	-isti	-ris
He/she/it	-t	-it	-tur
We	-mus	-imus	-mur
You (plural)	-tis	-istis	-mini
They	-nt	-erunt	-ntur

5 You also need to be thoroughly familiar with the case-endings of nouns, mainly so that you don't make a silly slip.

6 Clauses that begin with the words *cum, qui, ut* or *ne* (and a few others) are grammatically self-contained. You can safely leave them until you have worked out the main idea of the sentence, but when you . . .

7 *Check your translation by reading it through*: if it doesn't make sense to you, then there will be something wrong with your translation. Latin is a challenging language but it was designed to make sense!

8 Treat comprehension questions as 'guided translations'. The questions will point you to the right part of the passage, either by giving you line numbers, individual words and phrases, or a key word in the question that corresponds to a word in the text.

9   The Literature papers are where the highest grades are won, because you will have prepared everything in advance. So, *learn your set texts* – or rather, make sure that you know what every single Latin word in your set texts means in English.

10   You will also need to comment on *language* and *style*. Focus on using your eyes to spot repetitions of words, alliteration and emphatic positioning of key words. Are there lots of question marks? If so, why is the author asking so many questions? Are ideas and concepts piled up one after the other? What is effective about the author's choice of vocabulary – does he use simple or obscure words? Or do the words he uses have positive or negative implications?

Classics II: Classical Civilisation

1   To succeed in Classical Civilisation, you will need to show the following qualities:

- *Knowledge* of the societies, cultures and literature of the classical Greek and Roman worlds. What did they do? What did they believe? How did they try to make sure that the gods were on their side? What stories did they tell? What was daily life like?
- *Understanding* of why the Greeks' and Romans' beliefs and practices were important to them – why did they do what they did, and what did they think about themselves? *Comparisons with modern beliefs and practices* are often useful here (for example, Roman chariot racing was run along similar lines to modern F1, and the supporters of the individual teams were as fanatical as modern soccer fans).
- Some awareness of why *the ancient world is of relevance to us now*. What does the study of such things teach us about ourselves?

2   *Primary source material is the key to everything*. Everything you say, everything you argue, must be traceable back to some piece of evidence from the ancient world – whether it's a building the size of the Colosseum, or a passing reference in a literary text. Google and Encarta were not Classical authors, and using them as though they are definitive sources will gain you no credit – especially in coursework.

3   *Learn how to spell key words*, such as (in no particular order) *Colosseum, Caesar, emperor, Euripides, Eleusinian Mysteries*, etc. Many

of the technical terms you need to know and use confidently are fiddly, but an examiner will be more impressed by the candidate who spells these words consistently right.

4   In your Historical and Civilisation topics, learn the details and the definitions. If you have plenty of facts at your disposal, you will be able to answer most of the knowledge-based questions.

5   Most Civilisation topics are subdivided into manageable chunks – for Greek Religion, for example, you have gods and goddesses, prayer and sacrifices, important Athenian festivals, and how the Greeks tried to tell the future. *Break your revision down into these chunks too.*

6   Read and re-read your Literary set texts, so that you know the stories in detail. This will enable you to answer context questions such as 'What has Achilles just said?' and 'What happens next?'.

7   In the Literature papers, there are always a number of 'big themes' that underpin the set texts. Prepare yourself for the exam by writing the 'main theme' headings on a piece of paper and then write down a hot-list of events in the story which relate to that theme. In the *Iliad*, for instance, the main themes are: The anger of Achilles (from start to finish); What does it mean to be a hero in the Greek world, and is Achilles really such a great hero?; What does the Iliad tell us about the gods?; Are we supposed to feel sorry for Hector and the Trojans?; Does the *Iliad* glorify war?

8   Finally, and vitally, when you're writing your essays in the examination you must constantly think about *SEX*. Remember, you're being assessed on your knowledge of primary source material as well as the sophistication of your understanding, so you need to *back up every point you make by referring to a relevant fact* – an aspect of Roman bathing practices, or an episode from the literary text you have read. So, construct your essay by making a *Statement*, then *Explain/Evaluate* what you mean, and then give an *eXample*. See: Statement + Explanation + eXample = SEX!

Economics and Business Studies

1   *Mind maps.* Take a topic and branch out the key points . . . from these key points branch out any other points, e.g. advantages and disadvantages.

2   *Revision notes.* Use your notes and classwork/homework to make
    a concise set of revision notes – use basic mind maps, tables, bullet
    points here. Some might find different coloured pens etc. help to
    picture what is in the notes.

3   *Active recall.* Can you put your revision notes away and recall what
    is in them?

4   *Essay plans.* Take an essay title and *plan out* the 'route' of your
    answer.

5   *Evaluation.* Practise simple examples, e.g. evaluate the relative merits
    of chocolate to apples, and then apply to your subject question.
    Definition, pros and cons of each, personal judgements justified.

6   *Do not* just sit and read a book or notes. *Do something with them*
    from the above points.

English

1   Remember that *your own detailed knowledge of your set texts is
    absolutely crucial.* If you know your books then you'll be able to
    think for yourself. Don't rely on second-hand (and, very possibly,
    second-rate) ideas culled from study guides/the internet. Trust in
    your own ideas and responses.

2   Whether working on a major essay at home or producing the goods
    in the exam hall, *plan your time wisely.* Make sure that you allocate
    your time sensibly so that you don't leave yourself short of time
    at the end. Rushed work rarely produces satisfactory results.

3   *Know the task*: ask yourself what you are being asked to do.

4   *Pay very close attention to textual detail,* weaving short quotations
    into your sentence structure where appropriate.

5   *Develop your points as thoroughly as you can* and *focus upon how
    language is used* by the writer. (*Never* allow a quotation to speak
    for itself).

6   *Produce a clear structure and a coherent argument* in response to
    your title. The opening sentences in every succeeding paragraph
    are good points to show how your discussion is progressing.

7   *Retain a close fix upon your title* throughout your answer (including
    – and especially – in your conclusion).

8   Try to ensure that introductory and concluding paragraphs are
    precise, detailed and, above all, *worthwhile.* Avoid bland and general
    introductions/summaries, which do little 'work' other than eke
    away time and waste ink.

9   Have the confidence to *present your own opinions.* Remember that
    differing critical viewpoints – provided that they are supported by

textual evidence – make English such a fascinating and rewarding subject to study.

10 *Do your best to write with enthusiasm and sparkle.* The chances are that if you've engaged with your texts and *enjoyed* them, you'll write in a persuasive way.

Geography

1 Make a *progressive* summary of each topic in each subject.
2 Email your teacher with queries *as they arise.*
3 *Summarise your summary at least twice* before each class test.
4 Collate your skeleton summaries before end-of-year examinations and copy them out.
4 Reading does not represent 'study' – *you should actively make notes.*
5 Plan every response (short or extended) to questions *before* you commence writing – *allow time for some 'mental word-processing'.*
6 Plan essays first and write them last (i.e. do some other part of the exam while your sub-conscious mind dwells on the essay plan).
7 Answer the question asked and do not be lured into trying to impress the marker with 'related' material.
8 Field trips are very valuable in terms of hands-on experience: use them to the full.
9 Use the Examining Board's mark schemes your teachers will provide.
10 Buy yourself a 'floating ball' pen (i.e. one that allows you to write quickly without your forearm suffering from fatigue).
11 Sharpen your coloured pencils!

Maths

You need to remember computers come with manuals – brains don't! Mathematics is very much a subject that needs *constant re-visiting,* and students can do well provided they have done a *lot* of examples. *Repetition & Practice* is a marvellous learning method.

1 *Be positive.* This is a big key to revision. Don't let yourself think negative thoughts about your studies.
2 *Practice, practice, practice* for each topic. The main problem will be knowing where to start:
   • Your revision programme should be viewed as a series of small tasks.

- Decide on your overall revision schedule and then map each small task onto it.
- Prioritise – list the topics to be revised and rearrange the list in order of importance.
- *Don't waste time revising topics that you know well!*
- When you have decided on an area of revision, e.g. Trigonometry:
  - use worked examples in books;
  - highlight questions in past papers;
  - use computer revision programmes.
- Aim to do a certain amount of work at each session and *stop* when you have done that work. If you don't do that, you will always have more work to do and this becomes disheartening!
- *Monitor your progress.* Test yourself regularly to make sure that the topics are sinking in, or that you understand the topics.
- Answer questions without your notes in front of you!

3   *Use mnemonics* for remembering lists, formulae and spellings. For example:
- for the topic of trigonometry – SOH CAH TOA or Silly Old Hitler Caused Awful Havoc To Our Armies;
- for the topic of probability – **SAND***TIME*R (the word 'and' means multiply) and 'I *ad*ore probability' (the 'ad' of *ad*ore signals addition);
- for the spelling of ISOSCELES – I Sat On Swanwick's Chair Eating Lovely Egg Sandwiches;
- for area and circumference of circle formulae:

  > Tweedle dum and tweedle dee,
  > Around the circle is pi times d,
  > If the area is declared,
  > Use the formula pi r squared.

4   *Images* – the brain remembers images better than words – the use of colour helps – treat yourself to stationary to make learning more fun.

5   *The most difficult bit is always getting started* . . . but it is surprising how much easier it is once you *have* started! Once students have made a plan and organised their work, they normally start to feel pleased with themselves and want to move onto the revision.

6   *Do some revision every day to keep up the momentum.*

Modern Languages

All of the following implies regular learning and practice – grammatical concepts and forms, vocabulary.

Listening and reading

1   Listen/read for *gist* – do not be over-concerned with detail on first hearing/read-through.
2   *Be guided by the questions.* Use them to form expectations – what kind of notion does the question want you to focus on?
3   Don't be put off by 'red herrings', i.e. don't react to the first apparently plausible detail you hear/see.
4   Be sensitive to the 'little' words: e.g. (French examples) *pas* (not), *déjà* (already) etc.

Listening only

1   *Practise.* Get recordings from your teacher or from some other source (there are various websites that include listening items, e.g. the BBC website – follow the 'languages' link).
2   Listening is a skill you can practise during 'dead' time, i.e. while you're doing something else of a mechanical nature – sorting out your file, doing the washing up(!) etc.
3   *Be patient: play, replay, replay again*: each time you will pick up something new and the connections thus made will serve you well in the future.
4   If you can obtain a transcript, that would be an advantage – if parts of a recording have proved elusive, look them up.

Reading only

1   *Use 'signpost' words* which structure the meaning of a sentence: (French examples) – *mais, puis, cependant, malheureusement*, etc.
2   Apply the usual reading strategies: use titles, photographs, captions, sub-headings, first and last sentences of paragraphs, the questions on the text, to help you break down the passage.
3   *Also use context* and what you know about the way the world functions! – most of the time the gaps in your understanding can be filled by an intelligent guess.

Writing

1   *Wrong approach*: decide in English what you want to say and then go looking for the foreign language forms. *Do not think in English.*
2   *Right approach*: do a plan – make language notes: start with the language you *do* know and, with a little imagination, make it fit the given task. (Briefly put: don't work from the idea towards the language; start with familiar language and work towards the idea. *Display what you do know, not what you don't.*)
3   With this in mind, make a list in advance of useful structures – connecting devices, phrases, topic-specific vocabulary – and learn it well.

Oral

1   *Planning is critical.* Do your thinking in advance – you know what the likely questions are, so prepare good answers and rehearse them.
2   *Rehearse aloud.*
3   *Initiative is rewarded*, therefore try to offer a little extra detail spontaneously – say not just what you did, but where, how, when, with whom, maybe even why.
4   Get into the habit of *offering an opinion* and learn at least three or four ways of expressing it.
5   Learn a few simple devices for *connecting ideas*: e.g. (French example) explaining (*parce que, puisque, car, comme*); contrasting and qualifying (*cependant, par contre, en revanche*); sequencing in time (*d'abord, puis, ensuite, plus tard, après ça, finalement*).

Learning vocabulary

Learning must be *active*:

1   Cover the English words;
2   then cover the foreign language words;
3   *write the foreign language words down* (don't just look) – check and compare.

Physics

1   *Master and recognise the mathematics and algebra required.* At GCSE manipulation of the type of equation $a = b/c$ to make c or b the subject of the equation is absolutely essential. For instance, Newton's Second Law is $F = m \times a$ so $a = F/m$. At A Level, you

will encounter similar kinds of equations but containing squares and square roots.

2   *Obtain a good revision guide* and read and highlight difficult areas. There exist recommended revision guides for GCSE (CGP books), A-Level (Oxford Revision Guide) and IB (the school supplies the standard IB revision text to all Physics IB pupils).

3   *Obtain past papers* and work through and recognise the style of question, making particular note of the mark schemes. There are big differences between 1, 2, 3 and 4 mark questions. Find out what they are from teachers.

4   *Learn to sequence your thoughts* such that in answering questions, you state how A leads to B leads to C leads to D.

5   *Obtain a copy of the syllabus* and highlight all your problem areas. Work on these areas using text books and if possible ask older pupils or teachers.

6   *Produce or obtain a set of key equations and phrases* and write on postcards, reading them regularly and adding to them as each new topic comes along.

7   There are excellent revision sites on the internet, as well as quick tests and learning tips. Use these to supplement but not replace your normal studies. Type specific topics that are problems for you into a good search engine such as Google. Use Physics-specific words to narrow your searches. *GCSE Bytesize Physics* is an excellent site and there are many more like it.

8   *Take an interest in what you are learning.* If you are learning about infra red, then find out why it is causing global warming, find out about infra red remote controls, why firemen use it to find people in smoke, why we use it for computers to talk through optical fibres, why we use it for night vision. Howstuffworks.com is an excellent site for anything technical and applied that comes up in Physics.

9   Whenever you cover a difficult topic in school, use your textbook to follow up reading in the evening and *add extra notes to the notes that your teacher gave to you.*

10 *Ask questions and contribute in class.* Use your initiative and try to enjoy the subject.

Religious Education

Essay plans

A simple essay plan in an exam should consist of lines of argument that directly answer the question. *The plan should take no more than five minutes* and the rest of your essay should flow from them. They can then become the opening sentences of each paragraph.

Paragraph plans

This might seem like writing by numbers or writing to a formula but it gives a lot of scope for creativity within the structure. I often draw a rainbow on the board starting at the bottom with the opening sentence at the base and building up the elements of the paragraph in different colours.

1 Start each paragraph with a line of comment that *directly answers the question.*
2 Explain your argument more fully.
3 Give an example or piece of evidence/quotation to prove your point.
4 Give a counter argument or alternative point of view. Perhaps use another example.
5 Give a concluding comment that answers the question – hopefully *your own insightful opinion.* You might *'signpost' the argument* for your next paragraph.

After a while good habits like answering the question set, using examples, making comparisons and giving your own opinion become second nature and the structure can become less rigid. It is good to let students hear each others' sample paragraphs or to work in groups.

Once the basic skills are acquired then more sophisticated elements of good essay writing such as advanced vocabulary, the use of quotations, the views of scholars or historical considerations, can be built into the essay writing.

Opening and concluding sentences

A good exercise is to write opening and concluding sentences for a paragraph. It is possible to do this for a whole essay and make it flow like a piece of continuous prose.

Author's postscript

There is plenty to absorb and to build on there. So much so that I suggest you read through this chapter once again before moving on to Chapter 4, which is my commentary on, and exploration of, what you have just read.

Chapter 4

Exploiting it
Top tips commentary

At the end of the introduction to the comprehensive survey that comprises Chapter 3, I suggested you looked for 'endorsing repeats' as you went. How many did you find?

Actually, I made it easier for you: although some of the highlightings were those of the original authors, the majority are my editorial ones, looking to draw attention to that prodigious 'common ground' I cited in Chapter 1. And as you may also have noticed, it's not just that common ground which is prodigious: so is the *number* of qualities, skills and techniques recommended. Here's the list I compiled as I annotated the separate entries as I received them:

Attention to detail	Intensive repetition
Practise	Precision
Revising as you go	Grammar and spelling
Mnemonics	SEX!
Planning	Instructional verbs
Consistent focus	Learning and using technical terms
Alert editing	Logic and sound sequencing
Clarity of structure	Method 'versus' the answer
Analysis and comment	Individual opinion and view
Non-barrier thinking	Comparative thinking
Thinking in pictures	Enthusiasm/active engagement
Definition 'versus' valuation	

and

You are in charge of your learning.

Or, in short and in sum:

> At all times and in all respects, show that you fully know what
> you're talking about, what you're doing and why you're doing it.

That is a pretty imposing injunction! No less imposing is the list itself:
two dozen different concerns, requirements and goals – and I wouldn't
even claim it is comprehensive. Of course, more than several of those
twenty-four are closely connected and you can tackle them simultaneously. But they still warrant separate attention, for each needs to be
absorbed and then actively applied.

Attention to detail

Utterly fundamental – hence its place at the head of the list. You'll see,
I'm sure, that this essential need to master the little things, the
individual components of this structure or argument, that instruction
or governing method, informs a good many other things logged on
that list. Successful study depends on moving from the particular to
the general: don't try to do too much too fast, but master each stage
as it appears. That is coherent and it will quickly give you momentum;
as the erstwhile Chinese leader Mao Tse Tung observed: 'Every great
journey begins with a single step'.

Intensive repetition

It might be thought that this particularly applies to learning a new
language, and it is rightly emphasised in the modern languages entry.
But, in fact, nearly all learning is intensive: there is no greater aid to
memory than *frequency of encounter*.

That is very good news for those for whom this book was written.
It is often said – I have done so myself in other books – that the easiest
things to remember are those we are interested in (which is why we
all recall so much about ourselves!), and that is true. But intensive
repetition/frequency of encounter works just as well in the end;
moreover, once it has, you'll find it has *become* interesting, because it
is something you know and have achieved. So if you need to store
information of any kind that is resistant, attack it in short, intensive
bursts: make it *yours*.

As an example: I have a colleague who, faced with a not very bright
and pretty uninterested French set, devised a kind of game where the

pupils had to recite certain phrases or idioms three or four times, very rapidly. (One of them was the French for 'ground floor': *rez de chausée*, whose triple repetition has, as I found when I tried it myself, a satisfying and memorable rhythm.) Constrained at first, they eventually started to enjoy it, especially when the teacher spot-nominated them to recite a phrase of her choice. And by the end of the lesson:

> The whole class had memorised almost all the phrases in question; they had also had fun – good-hearted mutual teasing fun at times, yes, but also the fun of being actively involved in an apparently crazy game.

As I've stressed from the Preface onwards, having fun is the greatest of all helpmeets to successful study.

Practise

(Note: the noun – in the UK anyway – is spelt 'practice'.)
Much the same remarks apply as to the immediately previous section: the more you work at techniques (of whatever kind) the better you will become at them. The proverb 'practice makes perfect' may be a cliché and fall dully on the ear, but it is essentially true. The 'top tips' entries are full of excellent specific advice about this; all I'll add is that *you can't start too early.* Just as you should revise your work and add to your notes from the end of the first week onwards,[1] so you should practise new techniques and ways of thinking from the start.

One word of warning about practice, however. Be careful of doing *too many* practice past papers, especially as you near any exam. A wise former colleague of mine once observed:

> In the end, doing practice past papers makes you good at one thing only: doing practice past papers.

By which he meant that there's a boredom factor that can creep in, and also that however focused you might be on such work, you *know* it's only a practice. That is why mock exams are, finally, limited in value, especially in terms of accurate prophecy. They – and their other practice equivalents – are important in other ways, especially as *a learning experience.* But they are not 'the real thing', and for the latter you want to be fresh, hungry and still interested. Once practice becomes boring, it is worse than not any good: it can actually take you backwards. Watch for that staleness factor, and if you feel it creeping in, *stop at once.*

Precision

Precision is a close cousin to 'Attention to detail', both in wide-ranging importance and one-step-at-a-time focus. It applies to every subject, but I would say it is as much as anything a linguistic matter: if you are clear and precise about what you're saying, whether the language in question is algebra, French or English, you will almost automatically be taking good care of business. Always examine what you've just written; best of all,

> Read it aloud and see if it makes full sense to your ear.

If you think that seems a bizarre way to approach algebra or geometry, trust me: it works as well there as it does for an English essay or a practical write-up in Science.

Further: get into the early habit of making every word or symbol *do some real work*. Ensure that you know exactly what the words you employ mean, and look fiercely for any flab. Nothing you write should include these four (which I encounter far too often as an examiner at 'A'-level):

> sort of   definitely   basically   incredibly

which are entirely without weight, even meaning. But you should also be very wary of such leaden lead-ins as:

> It is interesting to note that . . .
> In order to do *x*, we must first consider *y* . . .
> It is worthy of note that . . .
> By way of conclusion it can be argued that . . .

Dull both to write and read, the key point about such structures is that they are *artificial*: no young writer would come up with them naturally or instinctively. They are the result of force-feeding by misguided instructors who consider them nourishing fodder, intrinsic to the health of your essay. They are nothing of the sort: they do no work, waste time and also irritate the reader. Leave them right out – and look hard for anything else that is bloated or joyless.

That last word is important. You can't *always* have fun when you're studying, especially if it's something you're not finding easy; conversely, though, you can at least avoid grinding dullness and mere toil. Try to *enjoy* putting things together with as much crisp precision as you can: you'll soon find it's rather nice to have written a clear muscular sentence that says exactly what you wanted it to, and the experience will be quickly infectious: you'll start doing it regularly, in time even automatically. And while I have latterly been concerned with the writing of continuous prose, the principles apply to any kind of focused work: getting things just right is always a boost, and confidence is a great enabler.

Revising as you go

In the Preface I offered a survey of how rapidly and strikingly study or key skills have evolved since they first surfaced as a discrete concept in the later 1970s, during which I observed that the one area that has remained stagnant is revision. If I seemed sour then, I'm going to be positively vinegarish now. For, very like Ian Sheldon's experience of hearing Chemistry rejected as hard or 'it doesn't run in the family', if I had a fiver for every school report I've read and every parent I've listened to that articulates a false, ignorant and often downright damaging grasp of what 'revision' means and how it should be conducted, I could contemplate buying a small Pacific island. Let's start with those reports.

In Chapter 2 I announced that 'It's not the teacher, it's the subject' is the biggest organisational lie you will encounter in the world of education. But a close second is this kind of thing:

> 'If s/he puts together an extensive revision programme and works hard at it every day, s/he should prosper.'

That's bad enough if it appears in the Christmas Report of an exam year, since it is starkly unrealistic and wrong-headed. Everyone privately knows that their pupils are going to do no such thing, or come anywhere near it. Nor *should* they, having just have finished a gruelling fourteen-week term:[2] above all they need a good, long rest, rebuilding brain and body for the rigours of the upcoming term, including of course mock exams.

To find such a comment contaminating an Easter Report is, however, even worse. If 's/he' really *does* need to embark for hours a day on a formidable revision programme, then there is only one inference to be drawn: the said 's/he' hasn't worked with anything like enough focus or efficiency during the last five terms, and the holiday needs to be spent doing not revision but *learning from scratch*. And that prompts the further inference that the teacher hasn't done a very good job in terms of monitoring progress and tracking genuine as opposed to imagined knowledge.

That is actually quite funny, or at any rate poignant. For probably the main reason why teachers roll out such useless and self-exposing bromides is that:

They are looking to cover themselves.

As I remarked in Chapter 1, teachers these days are under almost as much exam-pressure as the students in their charge, and I spoke of my sympathy in that respect, not least because I feel it myself. However, I have got a lot less – i.e. *no* – time for anyone who peddles institutional falsehoods and who in the process fails to enlighten pupils properly about:

1   what revision means and involves;
2   how it should be tackled;
3   when it should be integrated into a student's work programme.

The answers – well, *mine* anyway – are:

1   'a subsequent look' – or much better if not indeed obligatory, '*many* subsequent looks';
2   in short, sharp, specific task-focused bursts;
3   from the end of Week 1 of a six-term course.

Those three answers are absolutely of a piece with many observations made already in this Commentary and by my colleagues beforehand, and as I now introduce you to an acronym I devised some years ago – *RAYL* – it occurs to me that it can be re-coded to apply rather more widely than the purpose for which it was coined.

RAYL was a variant of the Inland Revenue's PAYE (Pay As You Earn) and signified

Review As You Learn

Needless to say, I still think that an important de-coding: it matches answer 3 above. But how about these versions to illuminate six items covered so far and still to come?

Intensive repetition	Repeat And You'll Learn
Practise	Rehearse All You've Learnt
Precision	Rigorous Accuracy Your Love

Consistent focus	Register All You Learn
Alert editing	Recheck And You're Laughing
You are in charge of your learning	Responsibility As Your Look-out

Some of those, admittedly, are more elegant or punchy than others, but the formula is an enabling one, I believe; I enjoyed putting them together, and you might find it fun and productive to construct some further variations for yourself.

Finally: if, as I and many colleagues advise, you do revise your work every few days – and it won't use up very much time – you will benefit in several ways. You will, obviously, re-enforce your learning; you will quickly realise how much and how fast you are learning, which will boost your confidence and thus sharpen your focus; and you should enjoy a very pleasant Easter holiday towards the end of the course, where your one remaining task will be to fill in the few gaps that will, probably, remain and to polish your knowledge in preparation for the *performance* that all exams involve.

Grammar and spelling

I've talked about these areas in both Chapters 1 and 2, so will add little here. At the time of writing they do not carry many marks in examinations, but to neglect them on that comfort zone basis would be foolish. Those who don't care about such things are invariably poor writers in other ways – awkward, often hard to understand, very evidently not in charge. Conversely, those who do pay proper attention to sentence structure and word accuracy tend to be, or certainly develop into, crisp and pleasing writers whose work is as telling as it is correct. And – sorry if I seem obsessive, but far too many students are injuriously lazy and/ or brain-mortgaging about this – be very wary of 'grammar' software (I haven't come across a really reliable package yet) and use spell-check to identify typos *and nothing else*. You need to check your own spelling in a contextual fashion, and there isn't a machine on planet Earth that can do that; I doubt there ever will be, because computers do not *think*.

Mnemonics

A mnemonic is a memory aid. It can take any form – a rhyme; an acronym which when fleshed-out will provide the exact information or principle that you want; a diagram or cartoon; anything that engages and pleases you. That mention of 'pleases you' is utterly important in mnemonics, and I'll be returning to it as we go, especially at the end.

There are some very good mnemonics in the Maths entry in particular, and that which concludes the Classical Civilisation one – *SEX!* – is *so* good that I have accorded it a sub-section to itself at the end of this topic! And of course, by all means take full advantage of those that your teachers may give you – *if they work*. They will not always do so; and I want to spend some time looking at why, and what you can do instead.

The first mnemonic I encountered was at primary school. Our teacher provided this sentence to help us remember the colours of the rainbow and the spectrum-order in which they occur – red, orange, yellow, green, blue, indigo, violet:

Richard **of Y**ork **g**ave **b**attle **in v**ain.

Obviously, it worked for me – hence, on one level, its inclusion here. But some fifty years later, a student of mine came up with

Rupert **of Y**eovil **g**rew **b**ananas **in V**enezuela.

An enchanting variant which enshrines a crucial point, or rather two points:

The most effective mnemonics are (1) Those which *amuse* you in some way;[3] (2) ones you make up *yourself.*

Here's a somewhat cautionary tale in support of that assertion.

Many years ago, in the course of teaching a class of (delightful and bright) eleven-year-old girls, I found that only a few of them could spell 'necessary'. That was no great surprise: everybody has trouble with the word – including me, for quite some time. What *was* a surprise, and an inspiring one, was when one of the girls revealed that she had learnt to get it right by using the sentence:

Never **e**at **c**hips: **e**at **s**alad **s**andwiches **a**nd **r**emain **y**oung.

Charming, concrete and very much the kind of thing which I thought girls about to become teenagers would instantly relate to, the formula impressed me so much that I urged the whole class to write it down and use it towards the next spelling test in a week or so's time.

That was a mistake. When that test was duly conducted, there was *some* class-improvement over 'necessary', but not the comprehensive one I was hoping for, indeed expecting. Then I belatedly realised why.

A mnemonic can only work if it is *itself* memorable.

Because *I* had found that sentence memorable, I wrongly assumed all would do so. Moreover, I had arguably made things worse for those for whom it hadn't worked: I had needlessly cluttered their brains with a jumble of half-remembered words, and they *still* didn't know how to spell 'necessary'.

So: try out mnemonics that you are supplied with, yes, but be ready to find your own structures and devices instead. Indeed, I would strongly advise you to do that anyway, for quite apart from the immediate gain of mastering something that was previously hazy, the activity will mobilise these vital qualities:

wit; creativity; active engagement; pleasure; increased control.

Once you have started to make those an ingredient of your study time, you'll be agreeably startled to find how quickly they can become part of *all* that you do.

As we near the end of this section, let me return to its opening paragraph. What 'pleases you' is a central consideration in almost all aspects of study, but it is especially so with mnemonics. Take stock of the things that make you laugh; the things that deeply interest you; the things you like very much and dislike very much;[4] the foods, drinks, music, films and television programmes you most enjoy. All such things are fundamental to your nature and personality, and if you activate them in your learning, you will rapidly benefit.

Don't look on such matters as distractions but as part of what you are as a student: get them to work *for* you.

One more example of my own to illustrate that, and then we'll move on.

For a long, long time I had a spelling block with 'dilettante'. The word means 'a dabbler, a flitter, a jack-of-all-trades but master of none', and it was a term I found myself wanting to use more than occasionally on school reports when attempting to get a promising student to become truly serious about his or her work. It was therefore very frustrating to have to look it up every time, since I could never remember whether it was one 'l' and two 't's, two 'l's and one 't', two of both, and so forth. And then one day I dreamed up this sentence:

> **D**on't **i**magine **l**ife **e**xists **t**o **t**ake **a**ll **n**arcotics **t**o **e**xcess.

That pleased me. You might think I'm very easily pleased, and that the sentence is a rather in-your-face one, and that, of course, is your privilege. But the real point for your purposes is that I created a structure which, because it pleased me, went right into my brain and stayed there: I have never since had to look up 'dilettante'. Don't copy that specific *example* unless it works for you, instantly and fully; I do, however, encourage you to imitate the *method* and principles which lie behind it.

And so, as promised, to . . .

SEX!

That acronym supremely exemplifies the value of fun, laughter and filth in getting your brain and your nature to work *for* you, not *deflect* you. The formula it logs

> **S**tatement, **E**xplanation, e**X**ample

is a sophisticated one in terms of how to structure a paragraph/ argument/essay, but I bet you now have a better chance of doing those things as a result. And take a leaf out of author Dr Paul Arnold's book: scholars are as dirty-minded as anyone else, and the best ones mobilise that fact, productively and joyously!

Planning

This will be a considerably shorter section – chiefly because, as with *attention to detail*, we've been addressing *planning* from the start of this Commentary, albeit implicitly or subterraneously. Every time you intensively rehearse your learning, planning is involved, as it is when you go about being as precise as you can, revising as you go, making sure your mechanical skills are in properly sound order, putting together your own mnemonics. All I really want to add to my colleagues' collective observations on the matter is this:

Planning is essential   Planning can be over-done

The Religious Education entry includes this sentence, which I high-lighted:

> The plan should take no more than five minutes.

I absolutely agree – whether the planning at issue concerns a prepara-tory essay; an exam essay; a schedule for your evening's work; a revision timetable; anything.

Like the closely-related *mind-maps* which several colleagues cite above, planning is an aid, not a goal in itself. The key thing, naturally, is the task itself; if you plan for too long, that bites injuriously into your mainstream work time;[5] it can even, insidiously, become what is some-times called 'displacement activity', which boils down to an excuse, subconscious or otherwise, for putting things off, for not getting on with the real stuff. Moreover, if you *need* to plan for longer than those five minutes, that probably means you're not truly *in charge* of what you're planning, and that you need to do some further preliminary work before you can tackle the task successfully.

The nice thing about planning is that there is only one rule: *does it work for you?* You can use mind-maps or their 'cousins', spidergrams; you can do it in word form, picture form, even doodle form; you can use all manner of coloured pens or a plain old-fashioned pencil; you can use a scrap of paper or create a state-of-the-art PC memo (though as noted, don't spend too long on that). And you can change the plan whenever you like or need to – a particularly liberating consideration when it comes to organising weekly schedules: the unexpected will always crop up from time to time, and you both need and should feel free to be elastic.

One last thing. A plan is a *guide*; it is not an *edict*. If you 'obey' your plan too rigidly, you risk ignoring a subsequent moment of inspiration or a new idea that comes to you while engaged on the actual task. I plan my lessons, naturally; however, if a student comes up with a perception or a question that doesn't 'belong' to my plan, I go with it nonetheless. It would be both stupid and unkind not to: it's the students' lesson as much at is mine, and teachers who ignore that or find any departure from their pre-ordained schedule unacceptably inconvenient are being a good deal less than enabling, however sound the lesson may be in essence. Analogously, be prepared to depart from *your* plan, to adjust it, even for a while to ignore it if what occurs to you pleases and energises. Like all aids, planning is a very good servant but a distinctly lousy master. It's you that is in charge: keep it that way.

Instructional verbs

I have included this material in three of my previous books in the Routledge Study Guides series. I make no apology for its cannibalisation here, because the topic is of the utmost importance to any examinee.

Well-motivated students who under-achieve in exams rarely do so because they have not prepared well enough or have been poorly taught. They do so because they misread questions, rush into things prematurely, go off at tangents, or all three.

It is often said that Exam Rule One is:

Do what you're told.

I agree with the sentiment but it should be Rule *Two*. As Rule One I nominate:

Do not write a word on your answer booklet until you are sure of what the question is asking you to do.

To be able to do that, of course, you need to be thoroughly at ease with all the various instructional or command verbs, and here are two exercises to help bring about that state of affairs.

First, Humanities subjects. The table below lists fourteen verbs and, alongside them, fourteen definitions. As it stands, not one such pairing is correct; can you effect fourteen 'matches'? The answers can be found in Appendix II.

Account for	Give reasons; say 'why' rather than just define
Analyse	Write down the information in the right order
Comment on	Item-by-item consideration of the topic, usually presented one under the other
Compare	Point out differences only and present result in orderly fashion
Contrast	Estimate the value of, looking at positive and negative attributes
Describe	Select features according to the question
Discuss	Present arguments for and against the topic in question; you can also give your opinion
Evaluate	Explain the cause of
Explain	Make critical or explanatory notes/observations
Identify	State the main features of an argument, omitting all that is only partially relevant
List	Give the main features or general features of a subject, omitting minor details and stressing structure
Outline	Make a survey of the subject, examining it critically
Review	Point out the differences and similarities
Summarise	Separate down into component parts and show how they interrelate with each other

Now, Science and Maths. The set-up and your task are exactly the same.

Calculate	Obtain the answer by extracting information
Deduce	Obtain the answer showing all relevant working
Determine	Obtain the derivative of a function
Differentiate	Obtain the integral of a function
Draw	Obtain the solution or root of an equation
Factorise	Represent by means of a labelled accurate diagram or graph
Integrate	Represent by means of a diagram or graph, labelled if required
Justify	Mark the position of points on a diagram
Plot	Show a result using known information
Show that	Give a valid reason for an answer or conclusion
Sketch	Obtain the required result without the formality of proof
Solve	Express as a product of factors
Write down	

Note: the final 'right-hand' row is blank because one of the definitions fits two verbs.

Those are hard exercises, and I can comfort you by saying: (a) that all my students, regardless of ability, need several re-visits before they are in complete control of all two dozen items; (b) that after all these years, having devised the exercises and used them so often, I *still* have to think long and hard about one or two of the 'matches' in question. And if you stick at it, most of them will become solid and secure in your mind before long. To repeat, though, in any exam, whatever the level or the subject, before you do *anything* else:

Decode all the relevant *command verbs*.

Then, and only then, you can start writing.

Consistent focus

Ian Sheldon's first Chemistry 'top tip' above is, 'Work out how you learn best', and that has a decisive bearing on this particular strand of our enquiry. For *consistent focus* hinges as much on coming to terms with your work rhythms and biological clock as it does, more obviously perhaps, on the need for concentration, mental organisation and alertness.

Let us make clear what 'consistent' means, or rather what it doesn't. It does not mean 'invariable'; it does not mean 'constant'; it does not mean 'unflagging'. Not even a towering genius is capable of that kind of focus; everyone, from Mozart to Mogadon Man, gets tired, has energy dips during any given day, at times feels out of sorts, suffers from Seasonal Affective Disorder, whatever. I admire my school very much and have been extremely happy there for getting on for a quarter of a century, but there is one thing about it that drives me crazy and which I wish it would summarily discontinue. On every school report, from Year 9 to 13, there are four categories indicating Effort, the highest of which is:

> Always gives of his best.

It is an absurd descriptor. *Nobody* gives of his/her best all the time: it is physically and mentally impossible.[6]

So don't feel you have to go down that biologically flawed, lexically sloppy route to achieve a level of focus that is admirable and will reap a fine harvest. You need to chill out occasionally, think about nothing much, even give your mind over to something that is silly or frankly junk. I often say to my students – and I mean it passionately:

> Anyone working at the kind of high voltage you generate most of the time needs to be a moron for an hour or so a day.

Of course, you need to be careful about that – two hours is probably too much, and bad habits are catching or can spread!

All that is a preamble to advising you to

> get to know thyself.

Socrates' injunction is desirable for all human beings, but it has a special bearing on those who are studying. Notwithstanding my scornful remarks above about 'always', you should of course aim at very clear focus as often as possible, be it a class or a period of private study. That will be much easier to achieve if your work-patterns are regular and their rhythm natural and comfortable. And to help you effect *that*, it will greatly assist you if the answers to these questions are firmly fixed in your mind:

1   Do you work best in the morning, the afternoon or the evening?
2   What is your normal concentration span when working on something you really enjoy and/or which comes easily to you?
3   What is your normal concentration span when working on something that is less congenial or which you find problematic?

4   How often do you look over your past work, and for how long?

5   How would you rate your memory?

6   Are you usually on time in submitting assignments?

7   Do you have enough time for rest and recreation?

In most cases, there are no 'right answers' as such; or to put it another way, the 'right answer' is the one you have given – *provided you act on it.*

Taking good note of the answers you've given will help you identify your strengths, especially those times when you know you're at your freshest, most energetic and most efficient: try to arrange your life so that your work sessions coincide with them as much as possible. Just as important, though, is that those answers also establish when you are at your dullest, least alert, least 'up for it'. Concerning those, we need to make a distinction between private time and those occasions when you're in class. The former is straightforward enough: as a general rule, it is best not to work at such times. For example, I hardly ever write between lunchtime and four-thirty. Regardless of what I've eaten or drunk, I have a noticeable energy dip then, and I know that not only would the stuff I turn out in that period be not very good: its mediocrity would depress me when I looked at it later, sapping my energy and confidence.

Class time is quite different. If you're stuck there in a low-voltage state, the temptation is to turn off at least somewhat and wait for the juice to return. It is easy to say this and difficult to do, but try to make an *extra* effort at such times. Even if you get only a little more out of the lesson than you otherwise would, that's still an advance on passive torpor; besides, you'll feel rather good about yourself for having at least tried to kick that sluggish brain into some kind of active participation, and that will strengthen your sense of achievement and well-being overall.

That august term 'circadian rhythms' denotes the individual biological clock that we all have; however, although the adjective means 'around or through the day', for our purposes we can extend it to the week, even to a whole half of term. Very few students (or for that matter, teachers) are likely to be at their shining best Period 8 on a Monday or Friday, for example. However, adopting the principle outlined in the previous paragraph, you could set yourself the challenge of

making sure you get more out of such lessons than anyone else.

A teacher friend of mine who had a pretty undistinguished set to teach on Monday Period 8 decided very early on in the year that she would make them look forward to that time as the *best* lesson of their week – an ambitious but splendid strategy (and judging from the eventual results, a largely successful one). You might fashion an analogous, almost bloody-minded resolve not to let those uncongenial times get the better of you. Even partial success will do a lot for your self-esteem, and for your overall 'consistency of focus'.

A final word about 'focus'. The human eye is a thing of wonder, but remarkable and multiple though its properties are, *it can only focus on one thing at a time*. It can *switch* focus with staggering speed and thereby absorb a great many things very fast, but it can only do so *singly*. Make that phenomenon a guideline for your own student behaviour. Don't try to do too much at once: focus on each individual item as it occurs, and be sure you've understood it before transferring your attention to the next one. In a way, that is what our first strand, 'Attention to detail', also means and involves: I told you these things overlap!

Learning and using technical terms

Jargon of all kinds is double-edged and as such will always be controversial. Over the years I have often heard it dismissed as 'too many fancy words', and it annoys almost all of us on that basis at times. After all, it ought to be possible to express any good idea simply and clearly; furthermore, if it *can't* be expressed simply and clearly, then it almost certainly isn't a good idea. That is a powerful argument, and in many cases it has a great deal of truth. However, as telegraphed, the matter is complicated by there being two kinds of jargon:

1   *Bad jargon.* Deliberately opaque words, terms and acronyms whose purpose is not to illuminate but function as a *secret code* which preserves the interests and the power of those initiated in it. Jargon of this kind is among the worst instances of language operating as a wall, not a window.

2   *Good or necessary jargon.* Terminology that might be obscure and difficult, but whose aim is exactitude and increased clarity, not sinister opacity.

As students, always be on the look-out for type 1 but only *use* type 2.

As you'll soon see, this is a short section; that's because there's a strict limit to how much general observation from me can be of use to you. Every subject has its own 'jargon', or to express it in a more aptly dignified way, its specialist vocabulary and metalanguage,[7] and you will learn these in your individual subject lessons. They take time to master, because they are sophisticated and, initially, strange; take that time, and don't use them until you're confident you've understood them sufficiently.

When you have reached that stage, there are two things I can say which I hope are fruitful. First, used appropriately, technical terms are extremely valuable in that:

1   they are absolutely precise, and
2   they save you (and your readers) a great deal of time.

In Chapter 2 I spoke of the absolute need for clarity, and how difficult, at times, that can be to achieve, especially when speaking or writing in English, whose very richness can often give rise to ambiguity. How comforting, then, to be able to use exact forms of metalanguage which cannot be misunderstood (provided, of course, that your reader is conversant with the terms you cite!). And their economy is no less a virtue: sometimes the deft use of a specialist word will save you a whole sentence. That will prove particularly beneficial in an exam, but it's a strength in any context.

Second, *never* use such terminology to show off or to give your work a spurious authority. If you use them sensibly and correctly you will look good, but if you use them chiefly *in order* to look good, such writing will almost certainly backfire on you. As I also observed in Chapter 2, nobody likes a smart-alec, and such people are very rarely smart anyway, just shallow.

Alert editing

Editing means two things here: immediate checking and considered re-writing. The second may well in time apply to you, but the first certainly applies to all of you, now. So the majority of this section is devoted to that former essential.

Checking over your work before you submit it is *nearly* as important as doing that work in the first place: not quite, but it's close. There is never any excuse for not checking over – fiercely – what you have written; moreover, not to do so sends very bad signals, both to you and whom-ever reads it. Those signals are that either you're lazy or you don't really care about anything you do being any good. Or both. It's bad enough that other people will think that: what matters even more is that *you* are living with that truth even if you don't recognise it, and as long as that goes on being so, you will always struggle and be deep-down unsatisfied.

Apologies for the mini-harangue, but I've seen what I've just defined manifest itself in the performance of hundreds, possibly thousands, of students, and I don't want it to happen to you. If there is nothing more depressing than to have a promising future *behind* you, then a close second must be the failure to use properly the gifts and skills you had when they actively mattered.

The much better news is that you can quickly and quite easily kick yourself out of such a reductive syndrome. Once you start taking proper professional care of business, the benefits are immediately evident, and the knock-on effects even greater. You'll start to feel a glow of pleasure at turning a just-about-okay piece into a good one; later – who knows? – that rhythm will become a case of turning a good piece into an excellent one.

Right, I shall from now on assume that you accept check-editing as essential. Now for some precise practical tips to make that final stage of the assignment optimally effective.

1   Do *not* try to do any truly effective checking at once. Read over what you've just written by all means – it is a natural and (I hope) pleasurable thing to do; however, such immediate perusal doesn't even begin to approximate proper checking, just as mere reading cannot remotely compare with reading-&-noting.[8] You will be tired after completion, and therefore at less than your best. Moreover, because the work will be freshly fizzing in your mind, when you re-peruse it shortly afterwards:

> You will see what you 'know' is there, not what actually *is* there.

That is especially true if you've done your work on a PC and are checking it on the screen, via hard-copy, or both. I know about that – oh boy, do I know about that! Virtually without exception, everything I write will have at least five typos per five hundred words, but I won't *see* them until the next morning. So, instead,

> check your work over the next morning

when you've slept, are rested, and your brain is newly alert. That's when you'll spot the mistakes and repairable clumsinesses or obscurities.

2   Yes, here I go again:

DO NOT TRUST YOUR SPELL-CHECKER.

Use it, fine; but you pass over control to it at your peril and almost certain doom. In addition, if you're a UK student, make sure the checker is set for UK English as opposed to American English. There's nothing inferior about the latter, naturally, but it is different, and it is very irritating to have bossy attention drawn to 'colours' or 'realise' which are, in the computer's view, erroneous; worse, it can erode your concentration, causing you miss *real* mistakes.

3   The same caution should attend presentation, fancy fonts, and so forth. Again, nothing wrong with these: on the contrary, stylish artwork and imaginative presentation will always enhance any assignment. But these things are secondary to the work itself, and focus on that should be your chief priority.

Two other tips – pleas, even:

(a)   Do not use any font size lower than 12.
(b)   For substantial pieces, use 1½ spacing, not 1.

Remember that your readers are older than you are (in some cases spectacularly so!), that they do a great deal of marking, and that eyestrain and brain-ache therefore constantly threaten. You make life difficult for them with minimalist font sizes and very closely-typed script. Pleasing, or at least not irking, the reader is an important consideration for any student who wants to be successful. And I'm not just talking about work that involves writing continuous prose: the principles I'm outlining apply across the board. It is very likely that if you deploy your work in English and French in an over-compact and arduous-to-follow fashion, the same flaws will attend your presentation in other subjects.

No less important – perhaps even more so – small fonts and cramped prose make it harder for *you* to read, check and edit your work. They also make it harder for your marker to annotate what you've done in a way that helps to take your work forward, simply because there's too little room to do so. Teaching and learning are like any other partnership: they form a two-way street, not a motorway.

Before we move on to editing in the *second* sense defined above, a final tip on the subject of fonts.

Choose one you really *like*.

An enormous number of students – and indeed teachers – settle for Times New Roman or whatever is the default setting on their system(s). That isn't exactly lazy, but it misses a trick, unless those default fonts truly please. As you write/calculate/draw, it is a significant bonus to enjoy the shapes and styles appearing on your screen as you touch the keys. It's yet another instance of making yourself *in charge*.

Editing in the sense of checking means, essentially, adding extra polish; however, the only thing you can polish is a surface. When it comes to the considered re-writing of such substantial projects as coursework assignments and extended essays or surveys, you'll probably need to dig deeper. That involves re-reading your work with a fiercely critical eye, which isn't easy. So:

> Try to imagine yourself as your marker.

You don't have to manufacture self-wounding hostility! Most markers, be they teachers or examiners, want your work to be good – it makes their job easier and more agreeable. But if something's amiss they're going to notice it and react accordingly, so get in first. Look for things which prompt questions such as:

> Is this sentence clear?
> Is this sentence necessary/does it do any work?
> Is this diagram clear and/or accurate?
> Have I set out this equation correctly?
> Are the tenses and agreements right in this German piece?

As I say, the process is not easy, especially to begin with; once under way, however, it's remarkable how much you can improve your work, and you'll find that any pain you experience of finding things wrong is superseded by the greater pleasure of having put them right.

For such extended work, you will invariably receive a good deal of help from your teachers. But it's worth getting a friend to look over your stuff as well. I've always been fortunate in my professional editors (i.e. those in the publishing houses with which I've been associated), but I've also been highly fortunate in my 'unofficial editors' – close friends whose judgment I trust, who in the main think well of my work, and who therefore don't let me get away with anything, so as to make it better. The increase in sharpness and precision is invaluable, and the sometimes intricate debates that attend the process are satisfying fun – not so much a bonus as integral to the whole business of successful output.

Finally: in such assignments, *word count* is invariably a key factor, and one that can cause a lot of stress. If you find you've gone noticeably over budget, don't immediately go into 'drastic mode' – that is, cutting whole paragraphs just like that. You might ultimately have to do something along those lines; first, however, look for individual words or phrases that can more or less painlessly be extracted. Especially, you might:

> Look at every adjective, adverb and other such qualifiers. Do you *really* need each one?

Sometimes the answer will be 'yes'; more often, given that you've got to make some sacrifices if you're going to meet your target, it will be 'no'.[9]

Once launched, this 'weeding operation' can also take in larger phrases and, if necessary, whole sentences: by now you will have a sharpened feel for what you want to say and the crispest, most telling way of saying it. And you'll be amazed how many words this thinning process will add up to – I always am, still. That excision of whole paragraphs may not be required after all.

That brings us to the half-way stage in terms of items covered; however, the rest of this commentary is very much shorter. That is partly because much of what there is to say about the remaining dozen items has been implicitly covered in their predecessors, and it might therefore be a good idea to have another look at those before reading on.

However, the relative brevity of what now ensues is also because I've 'banded' the remaining topics – which are more broadly conceptual than the skills-focused ones covered so far – into three mini-groups:

Band one:

    13 logic and sound sequencing;
    14 clarity of structure;
    15 method 'versus' the answer;
    16 analysis and comment;
    17 individual opinion and view.

Band two:

    18 non-barrier thinking;
    19 comparative thinking;
    20 thinking in pictures/images.

Band three:

21 enthusiasm/active engagement;
22 you are in charge of your learning;
23 definition 'versus' evaluation.

That arrangement allows us to focus on each item while simultaneously exploring their considerable thematic overlap and nourishing inter-relation.

Band one

If you get *Logic and sound sequencing* right, you will largely be taking care of *Clarity of structure* at the same time. Any assignment is analogous to a car journey. You plan it; you work out the way-stations and important junctions; you are (of course) mindful of the eventual destination, but first you've got to cover the ground in the most efficient and enjoyable way possible; that last also means that you need to keep your mind on your driving and each section of the road which you cover. Or to repeat the words of the Physics top tips entry in Chapter 3, 'A leads to B leads to C leads to D'. Unlike the driver, you also have to state, or at least clearly show, why that unfolding is logical and illuminating, but otherwise the analogy stands up well. You might encounter a mini-jam or some untidy construction work along the way, but if you patiently negotiate those and maintain that clarity of structure overall, you'll get there in the end.

Mention of 'end' brings us to *Method 'versus' answer* and *Analysis and comment*. Your conclusion/solution/overall 'take' are of course important: they govern your assignment, just as the destination of your journey governs everything you do before you reach it. But just as all the real *work* goes into the journey itself, so the major substance of your performance – and to strike a mercenary but vital note, most of the *marks* – have to do with your methodological activity (or 'working', as the mathematicians would say) and your analytical prowess.

Concerning those last two items further, you must not worry about whether your 'answer' will meet with the marker's approval. That issue doesn't really arise in Maths or Physics, say: in a final sense, it's either right or wrong. Even in those disciplines, though, your main task, and also your main pleasure, should be to arrive at that finale in a way that is clear and to your liking. And that brings in the final item in this Band, *Individual opinion and view*.

In all subjects that require you to argue, you must say what you think, not what you imagine 'they' want you to say. Relevant here is a passage from another novel by C.P. Snow:

No one minds what a man of distinction thinks.[10]

By this the speaker means that if you've got sufficient grounds and authority for what you say, 'they' will listen: whether they agree is not the point.[11] So when *analysing* and *commenting*, don't be shy: be honest. And be confident that your opinions and views are interesting precisely because they are individual. That, in turn, should ensure that you are always saying or showing something that has substance and that is *yours*. With that in mind, let's consider what *analysis* means and involves and how, done properly, it promotes that individuality.

When one analyses something, one strips it down to its individual components, examines each one, and then reassembles them into a restored whole. That applies as much to a poem as to a quadratic equation, a climate graph as to a painting; the process also exactly characterises re-conditioning a car engine, a recipe for paella or Hungarian goulash, or servicing a domestic boiler. It is a matter of careful and precise deconstruction leading to eventual enhancement. As you go through each stage, make sure your *comments* are not mere anonymous descriptions of what's in front of you but show that you have understood each aspect in its own right and where it 'fits'. That applies as much to Chemistry and Physics as to English and History.

All four topics in this Band hinge on the ability to relate the specific to the general, the individual details to the overall picture. If you approach your work with that pattern firmly in mind, it will all fall into place, be clearly communicated, and cogent throughout.

Band two

Non-barrier thinking, *Comparative thinking* and *Thinking in pictures/ images* all centre on one controlling and highly desirable property: elasticity of mind and an openness to learning as a whole, not in artificially isolated segments. I rather hate the modish term 'thinking outside the box', but if it helps you to get out of a conservative passive rut, that's fine by me. The term signifies (I assume) the ability to decompartmentalise, to look wherever possible for connections,[12] to avoid tunnel vision and, instead, look to learn everywhere, from everything and everyone. The 'top tips' have given you the best possible start in this, I hope: their common ground shows you that in most respects, learning is learning is learning. The territories may be specific, but they join up to make continents and indeed a globe.

Concerning the third: in my experience – from talking to any number of people, students of course included – the great majority of people do think in pictures, not in words. The words come later, when one has processed the initial and immediate images which illuminate our minds when we respond and think. Use that basic biological fact. Train yourself not just to register the pictures but use them as a fertile base. That applies to mnemonics – all the best memory aids are pictorially vivid, and the more dramatic/funny/filthy you can make them, the better! – but it holds true of all mental activity. And as your thinking becomes more sophisticated and you deal increasingly in abstract concepts (morality, evolution, relativity, harmony, discord, beauty . . . and so, almost endlessly, forth), see what picture or image first occurs to you when this or that concept comes into play. You'll be surprised at what does come into your mind, but you'll also be gratified and even delighted at what it enables in the way of focused concentration and the ability to deal more confidently with it.

Band three

This final section comprises just two paragraphs. That is not because *Enthusiasm/active engagement* and *You are in charge of your learning* are unimportant matters: on the contrary, they are fundamental. If both apply, for most of the time if not throughout, you will unquestionably be an effective student in all the other areas we have been examining. If in addition you are comfortable with the distinction between *definition* and *evaluation* – that is, on the one hand recognising objectively and dispassionately the formal properties and structures of whatever you're dealing with, on the other working out what you think of it, whether it convinces or looks/sounds right – you will be a student of true acumen, judgement and conviction.

So why I have left them till last? First, to serve as a kind of umbrella confirmation of what most energises success; second, to serve as a 'bridge' to the next chapter. For these three final concepts lie at the heart of Critical Thinking, a discipline which is both instructive fun and an assured way of sharpening your mind in all respects, and going beyond mere information-absorption into true knowledge.

Chapter 5

Sharpening it
Beyond information

PRELIMINARY

My initial conception of this chapter hinged on a truly remarkable recent development in the UK curriculum. Critical Thinking (CT), a course in informal reasoning and quite distinct from Philosophy and Logic, was introduced as an AS level (Lower Sixth) Examination Syllabus in 2003 by the OCR Board.[1] By 2007 it had become the single most populous AS choice – more entries than English, Maths or any science. Given that, it is quite likely that your own school offers it to its students, so you may be at least vaguely familiar with it already.

My own school has not yet adopted CT as an exam subject, but we do run courses on it for Year 11 and above. Students have enjoyed them and quickly benefited: one cannot take part in a CT class without being actively engaged, and that has a rapid knock-on effect in their mainstream work. That's why I had thought to explore it in some detail in this book: it seemed a highly enabling topic for those looking to improve less-than-strong performance in such mainstream work. On the other hand, the discipline is not only new but quite complex, and it proved difficult to cover adequately in a single chapter.

So this chapter is a lot shorter than its original draft. Any disappointed reader will be overjoyed, I'm sure, to know that Routledge have asked me to do a separate volume on Critical Thinking, to be published in 2009!

What this chapter now offers instead is some analogous thoughts on *metacognition*.

That technical term may look forbidding, but it is actually very simple: it means

thinking about thinking.

At a basic level that is what the successful student is doing all the time. And further to persuade you that the activity is a highly worthwhile one, I return to an analogy drawn towards the end of Chapter 4.

I talked then of the similarities between the process of writing an assignment and undertaking a substantial car journey – planning your route and taking early note of the important stages to come; being ready for temporary blockages or snarl-ups and having the patience and resourcefulness to overcome them; and of course covering the ground mile by mile/sentence by sentence. The destination, while of course governing, is only reached when all that prior business has been attended to.

Staying in the same area but varying the analogy: a route map cannot tell you how to drive, and the Ministry of Transport (MOT) certificate that ratifies the roadworthiness of your car can't get you through the driving test. On the other hand, driving is fairly pointless if you have no idea where you're going or how to get there, and even more – and dangerously – so if the vehicle you're in is not fit for purpose.

Metacognition can be likened to a brain-MOT. Directly and indirectly, it will test the various components of your intellect and hone them into full working order; it will recharge your mental batteries, increase the efficiency and power of your electrical connections, ensure that your gears are oiled and synchronised, and guarantee that you won't have a wheel come off. Moreover, it will mean that you are confident in your driving and that from now on it will be more comfortable and more fun. Or, to switch metaphors, it is the intellectual equivalent of going regularly to a gym: it might not make you fit overnight, but it starts and then mobilises a productive healthy process that will make you better all round.

ACQUIRING REAL KNOWLEDGE

> Becoming competent at a subject is much more than knowing a series of facts.[2]
>
> Roy van den Brink-Budgen

The limitations of 'facts'

As Chapter 3 (the heart of this book) stresses over and over, you won't get anywhere in any subject unless and until you master its basic information. Long before that – indeed, only a couple of pages into Chapter 1 – I quoted colleague Ian Sheldon's injunction:

Get out and learn the facts!

and of course he is quite right. But as Roy van den Brink-Budgen observes just above (and I know Ian would agree with him), if you want to do more than just get through, you need rather more than that:

Your aim must be to transform mere *information* into *knowledge.*

And the most enjoyable and productive way to bring that about is to

turn *facts* into something you can *experience.*

Pure information of any and all kinds is *impersonal.* You can register it, memorise it, recite it, write it down; you can do a great number of things with it, but unless you are a pronounced (possibly dangerous) weirdo, you cannot claim to *experience* it. Nobody forms a relationship with a train timetable, a menu or a bibliography, essential though those items might be as an enabling start. The journey itself, the dishes you consume and the book(s) you read as a result may turn out to be memorable, even life-changing experiences, but the raw data that initiated them are in a precise sense inanimate. A key perception in that respect – and again I make no apology for having cited it in previous Routledge Study Guides of mine – was provided over a century ago by William James, the first Professor of Psychology appointed by a UK university.

'Facts' themselves are not true. They simply *are.* Truth is the function of the beliefs that start and terminate among them.[3]

That is not easy either to 'decode' or then to assimilate. What it asserts is that the real significance of facts lies in how they are interpreted, how they are used by an individual discerning human brain. That is how people arrive at the 'truths' that inform and direct their lives, and they do that through the medium of *experience.* That is also how students progress from possession of information to active personal knowledge. And – a pre-eminently *personal* experience worth immediate investigation – it happens to characterise the forming of all new human relationships.

Getting to know you

When a newcomer joins a class, an organisation or a neighbourhood, we may have a raft of information about them via CVs, photographs, hearsay and so forth, but not until we meet them in the flesh does information about them start transforming itself into knowledge. And we can develop that embryonic analogy. Whenever we meet new people – of either gender and whatever age – we either decide (usually very quickly) whether or not we're interested in seeing them again and finding out more about them. Or, if they are going to be colleagues or people we will be *required* to see again, work out how we might proceed.

I suppose the latter scenario is more relevant to the student who, like it or not, *must* tackle this or that subject; nevertheless, in both cases some kind of relationship is embarked upon which will develop in some form or another. The process can be a very rapid one or much more gradual; how long it takes matters less than coming to understand the individuals involved, even acquiring intimacy with them. That unfolding might involve difficulties, confrontations, quarrels and *mis*understandings, but if the relationship is worthwhile it will survive such occurrences, even emerge the stronger for them. And at least those fractious moments are vibrant, for all that they might also cause discomfort and anxiety. In any relationship, the deadliest threat is *boredom*. Appropriately enough, given my analogy, it is also the student's deadliest enemy.

Avoiding the void

In Chapter 1, I observed:

> pupils are actually pretty good at dealing with boredom anyway, and they intuitively know that there's not much anyone can do about it

and I stand by that assertion. But at that point I was talking about subjects that pupils knew they would soon give up, and on which they would never be publicly examined; their boredom was an inevitable consequence of attending lessons bereft of meaning and thus inhabiting a kind of temporary void.

In all other student circumstances, boredom is not so much a consequence of the void as *the definitive expression of it*. For all the physical pungency of the phrase 'bored to tears', boredom is not something you can call an authentic *experience*. You might find that claim questionable in view of the obvious physical symptoms which break out – fidgeting, yawning, shifting around in one's chair, burying one's face into one's hands as one loses the will to live; paradoxically, though:

Those physical manifestations occur because the mind is empty; frozen; inert.

That's why we forget passages of boredom so quickly, and why, when people look back on their lives, they may vividly remember the good times and the bad times; the boring ones, though, have been wiped, and long ago too.

So, to return to and complete my analogy, just as almost anything in a relationship is better than long-term and endemic boredom, you as a student must keep that nothingness at bay, for boredom first disenfranchises and then obliterates. If necessary, *fight* your work, *attack* it, even *hate* it sometimes: at least it will remain yours, something you've engaged and which matters. However anguished and frustrating such times might be, you will still be making the transition from possessing information into acquiring knowledge.

There are other, rather more attractive ways of facilitating that, and to explore them I want briefly to consider what might be described as Critical Thinking's 'cousin' – the International Baccalaureate's Theory of Knowledge (ToK) component.

ToK: a brief introduction

ToK's explicit foci are:

- ways of knowing;
- areas of knowledge;
- the relationship between *perception*, *emotion*, *reason* and *language*;
- exemplary illustration.

To refer briefly to CT once more: that discipline is most concerned with *why* we think and argue as we do, whereas ToK chiefly focuses on *how* we think and argue as we do. Even so, the differences strike me as less significant than the inter-connections and similarities. CT rightly attaches considerable importance to structures, to logic, to underlying assumptions and to evidence. ToK might not spell such things out, but they are all pertinent to the way IB students develop their metacognition. When ToK students consider 'types of reason' for claiming or believing things – e.g. Value Judgment, Faith, Memory, Intuition – they are applying logic; they are examining assumptions; they are scrutinising evidence; and, inevitably, they are dealing with and fashioning structures, arguments and distinctions. Above all, they are – as the course's title would lead you to expect – investigating the nature of knowledge, its relation to truth, its varying forms and its varying media. It is the last two of those to which I turn now, in the belief that they can prove decisive in effecting those transitions that will establish you as fully in charge.

What types of knowledge are there?

It has been persuasively suggested that there are just three types of question.[4]

A   *Questions that have one, and only one, correct answer.* Put simply but soundly, such questions hinge on matters of *fact.* The chemical symbol for potassium is K, not 43; George Orwell's real name was Eric Blair, not Tony Blair; and erroneous arguments are *fallacies*, not *phalluses.*

All quizzes – from *Mastermind* to a pub evening in Middlewallop or wherever – traffic solely in such questions. Any quiz that even vaguely embraced the criteria discussed under (B) and (C) below would be impossible. It would last forever, or until such time as everyone got so fed up that they went home not knowing who (if anybody) might win the wretched quiz before death intervened – not a great recipe for a fun evening out.

I need hardly point out by now that I do not take a flippant attitude to basic matters of fact. I do want to re-emphasise, though, that while such information is the *foundation* of knowledge, it emphatically is not the whole *building.* Otherwise *Mastermind* would incontrovertibly mean what its title implies – that the ability to answer correctly thirty-five factually checkable questions means you are a great thinker. That is very obviously not so.

B   *Questions that have many possible answers but which require justification and reasoned judgements.* Two examples:

- What is the best way – is there indeed *any* way – to tackle the Middle East situation?
- How can we ensure that our children have a healthy and safe diet?

Any number of possible solutions can be advanced to either question. Some may be transparently inadequate; more than a few are likely to be cogent and worth taking seriously.

However, such richness of sound alternatives can itself create a problem: how does one choose which might be the most effective?

That is hard enough for an individual; it is much more difficult for a committee. Perhaps that's why so many obviously urgent problems take so long to be put right despite the concentrated good will of all concerned.

C   *Questions that have no correct answer but depend solely on the person answering.* An example might be, 'Which brand of cola tastes best?' My choice of 'taste' is deliberate, for answers to an enormous number of questions are, finally, a matter of nothing else. Taste is definingly personal and almost entirely subjective, whether it be literal or metaphorical, as in all aesthetic matters.[5] You can disagree profoundly with others' taste, you can even find them guilty of bad or appalling taste, but very rare are the times when you could call them *wrong*.

Any student is going to encounter probably thousands of questions of each type. One of the secrets of successful study and enquiry is to know the difference between them, and any others you might think of. Here's quite a challenging exercise to help sharpen that awareness.

Into which of the three categories do the questions in the table fit? You are not confined to a single choice, for you might decide that a number of them admit of two or more possibilities. You might also decide that you need further options, identifying a Type D or even E.

	A, B or C?
1 Which is the largest country in the world?	
2 Who is the British minister with responsibility for education?	
3 When was the First World War?	
4 Is it wrong to kill?	
5 What colour are your eyes?	
6 What colour is grass?	
7 Does God exist?	
8 Are we God's creatures?	
9 Are you well?	
10 Is your teacher well?	
11 Is two plus two always four?	
12 Does violence on TV contribute to violence in the community?	
13 Does rampantly irresponsible sex on TV contribute to rampantly irresponsible sex in the community?	
14 Do buttock-clenchingly boring documentaries, make-over and gardening programmes contribute to the growing suicide rate?	
15 Was Hitler a good leader?	
16 Can a male doctor know more about childbirth than a mother of ten children?	

That's quite a range of questions. Some will have interested or engaged you more than others; some will have seemed easy, others very difficult; one or two may have struck you as just silly. But in general – and this is the crucial point – they are much more debatable than might first appear. See how your responses compare with mine.

Commentary

Number	Type	Justification/Explanation
1	A and B	Apparently a simple A: the answer is 'Canada'. But since the question does not specify whether 'largest' is a matter of area or population, it could equally be regarded as a B. And in view of our earlier focus on the 'relativity' of truth, it's worth recalling that until the early 1990s the correct answer would have been 'USSR'.[6]
2	B	The question is not precise enough, and could be seen as fundamentally flawed. There are several ministers responsible for education under our current governmental system; moreover, it could be argued that the ultimate responsibility for the matter lies with the Prime Minister.
3	A and B	The simple answer is '1914–18'. But many would say it's too simple, ignoring the fact that in some respects the war continued beyond the 11 November Armistice. And while the first military engagements may have been in September 1914, those (literally) millions of people interested in the origins of the war might well argue that such a 'fact' is no more than a *local statistic*, the inevitable outcome not only of the assassination of Arch-Duke Ferdinand in Sarajevo but of a process that had been evolving for a very considerable time.
4	C	The question is absurdly vague for all its instant emotional impact. Kill what? Loved ones? Enemy soldiers? Armed would-be assailants? Cattle for human consumption? Fish ditto? Plants ditto? Flies? . . .
5	A or B	For something so basic to nearly all humans, *colour* is a maddeningly elusive concept. Many eyes are a subtle mixture of colours; even someone with unambiguously blue eyes might prompt debate as to whether they were sky-blue, carnation-blue, watery blue, and so forth.
6	B or C	Not A. Arguably the most stupid simile in English is 'as green as grass': there are probably over a hundred different shades of green that grass can have, dependent on time of year, locale and many other things. And of course a lot of grass isn't green at all: there aren't many colours it can't be or hasn't been.

| 7 | B, C or D | Again, not A: no human being can prove the existence of God (or His non-existence either). |

Initially I thought this a B; then, given that the issue is so much a matter of unique personal reflection, I tended towards C instead. But finally it occurred to me that the question is impossible to answer, which is my definition of Type D.

Note that, intriguingly, if the question were to be rephrased as 'Does the idea of God exist?', the answer would be a cast-iron A.

| 8 | B, C or D | All adjustments duly made, the same remarks apply here as immediately above. If forced to choose, I'd go for D. |

| 9 | A or C | If you take it to mean a routine enquiry about whether you're ill or not, A. If you dwell even briefly on the various possibilities signalled by 'well', it's a C. |

| 10 | D | The question is unanswerable by anyone other than the subject himself/herself. Even then it's problematic, as the second part of my commentary on question 9 suggests. |

| 11 | A or B | Most of us would plump for A, and with certainty. But some very good mathematicians of my acquaintance are less confident, so maybe we should all be cautious! |

| 12 | B or D | Certainly not the A that many believe it to be, but it can't really qualify as a C since there are only two possible answers, 'yes' or 'no'. However, I would personally say that it's impossible to answer to any satisfying degree: if 'yes', to what extent?/how directly?/so forth. The proposed relation between cause and effect is so tenuous as to be either meaningless or unrecordable, so this is a D. |

| 13 | B or D | This is essentially a spoof of the above. But it is not entirely facetious, for it underlines how suspect is the understanding of cause and effect that characterises wholly earnest questions such as number 12.[7] |

| 14 | E | E denotes a very silly question/one not worth asking. I hope this made you smile, but it has no value – or even status – as an argument. |

| 15 | A or B | Depends who you are and where you stand. The obvious answer is 'No' on an A basis, but it would not just be bigots or lunatics who would opt for B. |

| 16 | B | This question hinges on what precisely you take 'childbirth' to signify. If you understand it as 'the physical experience of giving birth', then the answer is of course 'No'. But if you read it as 'the science of obstetrics', then the answer will almost certainly be 'Yes'. |

It is surely significant that not one of those answers is an unambiguous A, and that even as an *arguable* type, A applies in under half the sixteen specimens. The exercise would therefore appear to bear out this assertion by the American novelist Norman Mailer:

> Nothing is more difficult to discover than a simple fact.[8]

It also points to the superiority of vigorous investigation over dutiful acceptance.

Justifying your thinking I: good reasons

The uniquely human activity of *reasoning* seems straightforward enough, signifying the capacity 'to think in a logical and controlled fashion'. Yet the reasons we have for thinking as we do are multiple; in addition, they are not all the product of what can properly be called reasoning. That does not make them invalid or even inferior, but it does, evidently, make them different. And since committed students are going to spend a fair proportion of their time arguing a host of cases across several separate subjects, it is important to be aware of the disparate types of reason that we have, how they work and when they best apply.

Below are twelve things which (for the purposes of this exercise) I shall claim to know, accompanied by the type of reason it uses. My commentary will follow, but as you peruse the list, are there any 'matches' which you consider questionable? Are there, also, any claims which could admit of more than one reason? And can you think of any further types?

#	I know ...	Type of reason
1	The grass is green because I can see it	Sense perception
2	$3 \times 3 = 9$	Logic
3	I have a fear of lightning	Self-awareness
4	I played squash yesterday	Memory
5	What the scientist said was true	Authority
6	Women are more emotional than men	Common knowledge
7	Exactly what God wants of me	Revelation
8	That my redeemer liveth	Faith
9	Beethoven is superior to the Beatles	Value judgement
10	I love my father	Instinct
11	It is wicked to murder a person	Intuition
12	It will rain tomorrow	Hunch

Commentary

#1 Sense perception

I don't think this statement could be defined as anything other than *sense perception*. I suppose it could be wittily argued that the reason in question is memory or faith or even common knowledge, but diverting though the discussion might be for a while, none of them stands up.

#2 Logic

Again, no contest. A couple of high-class mathematicians of my acquaintance have suggested that accepting '3 × 3 = 9' hinges on authority, memory or faith, but they were not entirely serious. Of course, what constitutes a number, the relations between numbers and also the status of the symbol '=' are all problematic,[9] but those considerations do not affect question 2's status as a logical deduction.

#3 Self-awareness

I can see why you might opt for *instinct* here. Any *phobia* is by definition irrational, whereas self-awareness implies careful, honest reasoning. But here the latter is the better choice precisely because of that: phobia it may be, but its existence has been absorbed and understood.

#4 Memory

An easy one. Needless to say, the memory can play tricks, and the statement could turn out to be wrong. However, that would not alter the *reason* underpinning the remark.

#5 Authority

The belief in someone's *authority* is of course a form of faith, and if you plumped for that here nobody could quarrel with you. However, a more or less unquestioning acceptance of expertise is a peculiar *kind* of faith, which admits of many things. Question 8 could not be considered a matter of authority, could it?

Incidentally, it is not remotely clear from this remark whether 'the scientist' has 'said' something about science: the 'what' could be *anything*! The appeal to or use of authority always needs to be weighed with great care.

#6 Common knowledge

However flawed and indeed absurd many such instances can be, it is a reason we all of us use at some time or another, and therefore needs to be taken good note of, if only for purposes of avoidance.

#7 Revelation

All sorts of things might seem to underscore or prompt this or similar *revelations* – acute self-awareness; faith; intuition; even a hunch. But the idea of 'mysterious visitation' central to revelation transcends all those, and that is surely the governing idea here.

#8 Faith

The only real contender, ultimately. Such a belief could be accompanied or prompted by revelation, yes; but that is not essential for the belief to be an unswerving and certain one. Please note that such certainty cannot be called knowledge. However much a devout believer might assert it as such, this is something that cannot be known: that, after all, is the whole point about faith and indeed its defining property.

#9 Value judgement

We indulge in these all the time. There is no harm in that, nor any call to despise this reason as a mere opinionatedness. Our tastes and views are fundamental to us as unique individuals who think, feel and believe, and it would be idiotic to 'downgrade' them simply because they can never aspire to factual status. The key to *value judgement* is to be aware that it is just that, however much it may incidentally impress as authoritative, apparently logical or even on occasion revelatory.

#10–12 Instinct, intuition and hunch

I've bracketed these together because:

1   They seem – and in some respects are – semi-synonymous, as these *OED* extracts demonstrate:
   a   Acting on *instinct* is 'to act without conscious decision'.
   b   To *intuit* is 'to know immediately without reasoning'.
   c   A *hunch* is 'a hint; an intuitive feeling'.

2   They are all seriously problematic as 'modes of knowing', being both very difficult to explain and therefore to justify. As a result . . .

3   . . . the examples I've provided do not, I think, *obviously* belong in the categories to which I've assigned them. That's not to say they are weak or wrong but to observe that when it comes to any kind of 'gut feeling', it is almost impossible to say what is driving it.

My hunch about the rain could, for instance, be down to memory or sense-perception – the look of the clouds, the 'feel' of the air; it could equally be a kind of *prayer*. Similarly, my love for my father may be ingrained instinct, but it could be the result of instruction. It might also be said that *love* is so rich, deep and complex a phenomenon that trying to 'explain' it in any way is both unnecessary and futile. And the *intuition* that murder is wicked could, equally, be an instructed notion that owes more to teaching than to feeling.[10]

It may occur to you that I've chosen a highly frustrating way in which to conclude a survey of why we think as we do. That triple-entry is not only indeterminate in itself, but seems to undermine the validity, or at least the precision, of *all* our reasons. Well, yes and no – but chiefly 'no', in that questions 10–12 confirm three vital things:

- How *similar* are many of our reasons, even though their range as an entire collection is formidable.
- In many instances we may have *more than one reason* for stating, believing or doing something.[11]
- A host of things that I/we may claim to *know* are not apprehended *cerebrally*. That emphatically does not make those things worthless; on the contrary, it suggests – irresistibly – that there is more to human wisdom and the life of the brain than can be attributed to the 'mere' power of reasoning. And amongst all else, that neatly sets up the final section of this chapter.

Justifying your thinking II: more on the 'hunch'

The *hunch* might qualify as a form of 'first impression' were it not that it often makes itself felt *before* one's initial look at something or somebody. Earlier I defined it as 'a gut feeling'; an analogous but brain-related term might be 'advance subconscious intelligence'. Both point to an intuition that arrives out of the blue before the forebrain has started its work.

Since it pre-dates any empirical or forensic evidence, it is tempting to see a hunch as the antithesis of scientific method. Yet the history of science abounds in instances of discoveries that began in instinctive belief. Here's an example furnished by Professor C.A. Mace:

> When Toricelli inverted a tube of mercury, thereby inventing the barometer, and when Florin Perier carried his barometer up the Puy de Dome to observe the influence of altitude, they did not do these things merely to 'see what would happen.' They must have had *a shrewd idea in advance.* Otherwise their conduct would have been eccentric.[12] [My italics]

The italicised phrase provides another definition of a hunch – a splendid one that can also be applied to the now-legendary work of Francis Crick and James Watson. When they started their laboratory investigations into the structure of DNA, both were already convinced its shape was a double-helix; all they needed to do was to prove it! It took them years, but they succeeded – and much later Crick had this to say about their procedures:

> *It is true that in blundering about, we found gold,* but the fact remains we were looking for gold – asking the right question.[13]

'A shrewd idea in advance'; 'asking the right question': both should be part of your armoury as you strive for those good, even outstanding, passes.

Conclusion

As I advertised at the outset, this shortish chapter has been driven by metacognition. I hope I have satisfied you that *thinking about thinking* is not only interesting fun but an activity that can only increase your ability to distinguish what is important from what is trivial; what is worthwhile from what is worthless; perhaps above all, what is sound from what is suspect. And any bright, hungry student needs all those awarenesses in full.

Chapter 6

Enjoying it

Happy students are good students

No profit grows where is no pleasure taken;
In brief, sir, study what you most affect.

Petruchio in *The Taming of the Shrew*

PRELIMINARY AND FUNDAMENTALS

Not all of you will yet be in a position to study only 'what you most affect' (i.e. what you most like), but Petruchio's overall message can and should be absorbed by any committed student. 'Pleasure' can indicate satisfaction as much as pure enjoyment – including, as I've remarked earlier, the pleasure of proving wholly wrong those who doubted you, yourself included.

But 'pleasure' involves other things too. Make sure that the 'inner man/woman' is properly catered for. That means following a sensible but enjoyable diet and refreshing yourself regularly with drinks of your choice (including water, naturally); making your working environment comfortable and congenial, including background music of your choice, provided that assists rather than distracts you; taking time out to enjoy yourself away from your desk – within reason, look to have a good time when you're off duty. And in addition, 'chill out' occasionally: your brain needs rest just as much as your body and soul do.

With all that and more in mind, I trust you will indulge me as I return to something I wrote a quarter of a century ago when composing an earlier Study Skills book. At its start I offered four 'Student Portraits', designed both to amuse and instruct. I rehearse them here – in re-written and shortened, bullet-pointed form – in the belief that they still have something important to say about pleasure, commitment, satisfaction and enjoyment – properties crucial to the successful pursuit of *anything*, including academic study.

1 *The would-be student:*
- Likes the *idea* of studying rather than the *fact*.
- Enjoys the prospect of success, plans the way s/he will build on it, but finds it irksome (if not alien) to get down to any real work.
- Expects the teacher to do at least ninety-seven per cent of the work.
- Hostile to exams – they're 'unfair', 'arbitrary', even 'evil'.
- Expends formidable energy finding 'displacement activity' reasons not to work. These are often brilliantly ingenious – but what might have been achieved if their inventor had devoted that same energy to mainstream study?

2 *The earnest student:*
- All mouth and notebooks.
- Anti-humour, fun or entertainment: ES wants to *work*, not take part in a comedy show: jokes waste valuable time.
- Teacher is God Almighty – until said person is (inevitably) proved fallible, whereupon s/he becomes a liability, even a menace.
- Demands everything be *relevant*: all things even slightly off the beaten track are mere chaff.
- A towering snob: Shakespeare is wonderful, but stylish light fiction won't do at all. Beethoven Rules OK; the Rolling Stones/Coldplay are noisy yobs – and as for that hideous hybrid *jazz* . . .
- May be able; may be not. May be vocal and aggressive; may sit in Olympian silence. But whatever ES's talent and personality, s/he is absolutely clear about one thing, thank you very much: *study is a serious business.* No time for digression, scepticism, tolerance of the non-serious, tolerance of most kinds: at root, in fact, ES is fascist.
- Expects to end up knowing all the answers; is not remotely interested in the questions.

3 *The admirable student:*
- Not a paragon; gets fed up and bored with study at times, and can have periods of total lethargy. That is entirely normal: s/he knows that and refuses to worry about it.
- Wants to learn; prepared to work at doing so. Accepts that what is asked in the way of reading and listening is to be taken seriously, but is not unquestioningly reverent.

- Prefers to be delighted and impressed, but knows rubbish when s/he sees it, and enjoys the much underrated pleasures of destructive criticism.
- Humble.[1] Neither afraid to be wrong nor determined to be serious all the time: knows that silliness and moments of moronity/utter inertia are important as diversions and leisure for the brain.
- Lives with study as an intimate pleasure; retains the quality of wonder that characterises the child.
- At his/her most impressive, resembles Benjamin Franklin's ideal of 'the wise innocent'.

4   *The lucky student*:
- A natural worker who likes lessons.
- Consequently, in early years often called a 'swot', and initially attracts hostility based on envy . . .
- . . . which s/he eventually disarms through cheerfulness and natural dignity.
- Does not always triumph; not necessarily *that* bright or 'gifted and talented'. But will *become* so through commitment to work: quantity changes quality.
- The 'luck' here is that of anyone fortunate enough to find an activity that enchants and energises.

I commented at the time that 'most students contrive to be all four types at different times: I know that *I* have.' But it is pretty obvious – isn't it? – that Types 1 and 2 are not going to be very successful (for different reasons), whereas Types 3 and 4 almost certainly will be.

You might not think of yourself as belonging to either of those latter types when it comes to the reason you're reading this book – i.e. in your weaker subjects. But you easily can be. If I had to choose one bullet point as definitive from all those logged above, it would be:

> Does not always triumph; not necessarily *that* bright or 'gifted and talented'. But will *become* so through commitment to work: quantity changes quality.

That commitment will be all the more natural if you are healthy, at one with yourself and generally enjoying your life. Naturally, you will have reverses (and not just in your studies), but surviving and surmounting those will breed both strength and confidence.

A further pleasurable way to progress and increase your in-charge control is to ensure that all your *mechanics* are precise and professional. By that I do not this time mean spelling, grammar and all the other things I discussed in Chapter 2 under 'Getting the little things right', but something rather more sophisticated. It deserves a section to itself, not least because mastering its contents will greatly increase your satisfaction and pride.

THE MECHANICS OF SCHOLARSHIP

At whatever level and whichever course you study, your chief concern will always be with the 'real stuff' of your assignment – the material, the argument, the discoveries, the conclusions drawn, and so forth. And rightly so. If that *core* is inadequate in any way, no amount of tarting-up is going to disguise that fact; for that reason alone you should delay focusing on presentational matters until you are solidly confident about the material you have drafted – which means towards the end of the entire process.

However, that is not to denigrate attractive and professional presentation. On the contrary, it is becoming more and more important within educational assessment; moreover, the International Baccalaureate Organisation (IBO) has recently observed that American students tend to be much better in this area than their UK counterparts, and it is safe to assume that this probably applies to non-IB students too.

If this section's title seems a bit intimidating, don't let it be so. What I'm concerned with here is:

- when footnote references are required or advisable;
- how they should be written;
- choosing between footnotes and endnotes;
- citing website references;
- furnishing a bibliography;
- composing an abstract.

My advice and observations are neither comprehensive nor fool-proof; different organisations and publications have their own 'house style' and you may have to adapt the models I have provided to fit in with others' specific conventions and requirements. But you are unlikely to be found seriously wanting in any respect if you follow the procedures laid down here.

Citing references – footnotes and endnotes

When references are required

Despite the stern tone of some of my opening observations, it is very important that you do not feel *bullied* about footnotes. Yes, they matter, but if you are panicked into adopting a kind of scatter-gun approach, you will do yourself more harm than good. You need to be sure that:

> The reference is necessary and relevant; it is not merely a time-wasting paraphrase but does some real work, moving your piece forward.

Naturally, you must *acknowledge* major sources if drawing on them in your own argument. But it is invariably a mistake to cite them in detail if they're seminal or truly renowned. Let us take two examples: Elton's work on the Tudors and Friedman's monetarist theories.

Any competent historian will be fully conversant with the former, any competent economist with the latter. You may therefore take such readers' knowledge for granted, and concentrate on showing how your knowledge of this work influences your own thinking. Reference to such sources can and should be crisp and brief: if you know what you're talking about, there is no need to prove it with a lot of laborious 'story telling', just as there's never any need in a literary essay to recite the plot.

How footnotes should be set out

First, the rudimentary pattern.

> Author > Work > Publisher and Date > Page(s) in question

That is a good foundation, but it is *skeletal*: most references will require additional fleshing-out. For example: some of what I'm writing here is adapted from the chapter on Essays in my book *Write in Style*. If I wanted to log that in footnote form, the reference would read:

> Richard Palmer, 'Essays', *Write in Style* (London: Routledge, 2002), 154–5.

It is worth dwelling on the need for accuracy in every last item there; please forgive the rather 'cat-sat-on-the-mat' approach.

- First, unless there are exceptional reasons for doing so, you should not cite the author's title – Dr, Professor, Sir, whatever. Given name and surname are all that is required.
- Note the placing of all the commas.
- Note too the colon between the *place* of publication and the specific publishing house.
- Note the comma separating the latter and the date of publication.[2]
- The title of a chapter/article is housed in inverted commas; the full title of the work is italicised.[3]
- You do not *need* 'p.' or 'pp.' before the page numbers. That said, some organisations/publications do make it part of their house style, so be ready to adjust.

Two further complications/elaborations, and then you should be fully 'armed'.

1   From time to time you will be quoting from a revised or subsequent edition of a particular book. The procedure in such a case is:

> E.H. Carr, 'The Historian and his Facts', *What is History?*
> (London: Macmillan, 1961). Penguin edition (1987), 12.

2   If quoting from a newspaper, the pattern is essentially the same, except that the place of publication is not required and the date is both differently located and exact:

> Glyn Brown, 'Elvis Remembered: A Gifted White-Trash Boy
> Who Trusted the Wrong People', *The Times* 2, 31 July,
> 2002.

Footnotes 'versus' endnotes

It is one thing to be meticulous and scholarly in your referencing; it is quite another when those very virtues turn into vices, or at least into irritating distractions. Too many footnotes can clutter up your work and start to irritate the reader. So if your assignment is going to contain a lot of references – and you should be aware of that probability before you even start writing – it is better to use a numbering system and collate such references at the end (which you'll have noticed is the practice I've adopted in this volume).

Citing websites

Nowadays, and one suspects increasingly, website referencing is as frequent as 'traditional' citations. Nothing wrong with that, naturally, but the practice has its own precise requirements, and no serious student can afford to be lazy about 'netiquette'.

First and foremost: it is not enough to cite something like www.factsforsadanoraks.com and leave it at that. Just as with books and periodicals, you need as full a provenance as you can supply – author, date and, if possible, page(s). The last might not be traceable or indeed useful, but the provision should still be borne in mind. Naming the author is especially important, and not just for mechanical reasons.

1   The best thing about the internet is that it is utterly democratic: anyone can publish on it. That is a wonderful advance in human freedom and potency, and it should be celebrated.

2   Paradoxically, though: the *worst* thing about the internet is that anyone can publish on it! You don't have to be an elitist to realise that this means a prodigious amount of junk is charging around the ether, and you need to exercise great discernment when contemplating net material for use in your work.

3   Therefore, a key test is whether there is any author identification. If there *isn't*, the stuff is likely to be dodgy and/or seriously inadequate; indeed, the chances are high that it is all rubbish.

Note: these brief observations focus solely on bibliographical procedures. A full consideration of 'netiquette' – Net practice – follows this section.

Furnishing a bibliography

If, or once, you feel comfortable about footnote procedure, bibliography should hold no terrors for you. Such entries are less 'fiddly' than along-the-way referencing; their chief purpose is to record, clearly and discretely, the texts and sources which have significantly influenced that which you have argued in your assignment.

As a model, here is an abridged version of a bibliography I composed a few years ago:

GENERAL		
Tony Buzan (2003)	*Use Your Head*	London, BBC
Guy Claxton (2000)	*Wise Up: The Challenge of Lifelong Learning*	London, Bloomsbury
C.A. Mace (1969)	*The Psychology of Study*	Harmondsworth, Penguin
Jonathan Smith (2000)	*The Learning Game*	London, Little and Brown
WRITING		
Bill Bryson (1994)	*Dictionary For Writers and Editors*	Harmondsworth, Penguin
Ernest Gowers (1987)	*The Complete Plain Words*	Harmondsworth, Penguin
John Kirkman (2005)	*Full Marks*	London, Routledge
READING		
Manya and Eric De Leeuw (1990)	*Read Better, Read Faster*	Harmondsworth, Penguin

I am not being condescending when I observe that at present it is unlikely that you'll need to cite as many works as appear above. But notice the *divisions* – into 'General', 'Writing' and 'Reading'. You may not *need* to separate your listings in such a way, but it can help to sharpen your readers' awareness of the range and organisation of what you've consulted, and that is always going to be to your advantage.

Composing an abstract

This causes even experienced students more trouble than any of the other tasks under consideration, and I'm not surprised. The term itself is difficult, and if the IBO's definitions and approach are anything to go by, it is also currently imprecise, even *vague*.

Right: a definition first. In this usage, abstract = that which has been deducted or removed. And, you may (rightly) think, a fat lot of help *that* is! So, more productively I hope:

> An abstract equates to a brief statement about what your piece centrally addresses and to what conclusion it has led you.

Note that, while it should focus on the question/topic selected and indicate in a nutshell your findings, *it does not have to summarise the interim arguments you employ.*

If you find that strange, join the club! But that's the way it seems to be – for IB assignments and others. The good news in the midst of so much confusion and strangeness is that:

In actual fact, composing the abstract is no big deal provided you've done the assignment well, fully know what it's about and what it adds up to.

But that means one thing above all others:

Even though it appears on page 2 of your submission, the abstract is *the very last thing you should write.*

Two last recommendations:

1   *Use the present tense*:

In this essay I consider [rather than *I considered*] . . .; Brown-field sites are a significant ecological and economic advance [rather than *Researching brown-field sites persuaded me that* . . .]

The present tense keeps your assignment 'live' and vibrant.

2   *Strenuously avoid all UCAS Box 10-style gushing*:

I chose this title because I have a passion for . . .

Actually, such style is bad enough in Box 10s themselves.[4] It is even more damaging – *and* word-wasteful – in an abstract, which (in IB circumstances if not others) must never exceed three hundred words and ideally might be noticeably shorter.

Three additional points

1   You can if you wish *avoid footnotes altogether* by using *in-text referencing.* You write out the chosen quotation in exactly the same way; then instead of inserting a foot- or endnote you simply cite, immediately afterwards and in brackets, the author's surname and the relevant page reference. To illustrate the technique, I'll return to the Richard Palmer and E.H. Carr examples which appear in the main document.

(a) '*A Study of Reading Habits* by Philip Larkin, published in 1960 . . . is a deceptively provocative poem . . .' (Palmer, 154–5). Then on with your own main text.

(b) 'The belief in a hard core of historical facts existing objectively and independently of the interpretation of the historian is a preposterous fallacy, but one which it is very hard to eradicate' (Carr, 12). Then on with your own main text.

Of course, this means that all such books and sources referenced in this way *must* appear in your bibliography under the specific subtitle 'Works cited'.

This technique featured in an article I had published three years ago: it was the mandatory 'house style' of the journal in question. And to be candid, I *hated* it. I didn't like it as a writer, and I like it even less as a reader: I find the consequent 'hurdles when reading through' (as a colleague deftly phrased it) cumulatively annoying.

That said, the option is a legitimate and recognised one, by no means inferior to the other two. Your best course is to elect the one with which you feel most comfortable and which in your view *looks* best. Whichever you choose, though, make sure every last detail is accurate and as it should be.

2   Bibliographies can be a poisoned chalice or an elaborate way of shooting yourself in the foot. Do not quote a whole list of sources simply because you think it 'looks good'. If you haven't read them, it will be obvious from your text – and that will look very bad.

3   Finally, concerning the abstract: a word about *style*. Further to ensure the absence of gush and/or an over-colloquial or casual tone, there is a lot to be said for expressing yourself in the *third person*.

(a)   This essay examines the recent growth in Brown-Field Sites and the ensuing impact on the local economy and environment. It concludes that this has been a mainly beneficial development, though some of the ecological consequences are problematic.

(b)   This survey explores the relationship between Shakespeare's *Antony and Cleopatra* and the period of Roman history it dramatises. While the playwright takes a number of major liberties, not least in compressing the action into months as opposed to the decade-plus in question, his play is faithful to the ethos and governing issues of the period even if chronology is sacrificed.

That might feel awkward and pompous at first, but it is a mode very well worth mastering. Its twin advantages are to guarantee dignity and to suggest scholarly objectivity in a fashion that 'I have always wanted to explore . . .' does not necessarily achieve.

Such an intricate collection of task-guidelines may strike you as rather at odds with this chapter's titular stress on *happiness*, and I will straightaway admit that logging footnotes, abstracts and other such ancillary matters very rarely inspires bursts of joy. However, taking care of such essential business can certainly be quietly satisfying, and the finished product will please you with its professional elegance and clarity.

NET PRACTICE

I'm a touch nervous about writing this section, mainly because you almost certainly know more about it than I. In the last five years or so, the net has become the student's main and most immediate research source; as a result, when it comes to website knowledge, efficient use of search engines and sheer technological facility, young users have left most of their teachers standing. Indeed, I have already learnt a good deal about such things from my own students, who in this instance are the professionals while I'm the amateur. On the assumption that you resemble them in that respect, I'm not going to waste any time telling you things you know already, and better than I.

However, I do want not so much to sound a note of warning as offer two cautionary (though positive) tips. The first hinges on two observations which I've outlined already but will now explore in proper detail.

The *best* thing about the net is that it is democratic

Naturally, many attributes of the net are worth celebrating. Five that benefit academics spring instantly to my mind:

1   Access to a world of information available without you having to move out of your chair, let alone out of the house.
2   The sheer speed with which you can engage that facility.
3   Being able to download desired material simply, quickly and cheaply. The previous alternatives were either laborious and slow (writing the text out by hand) or cumulatively very expensive (using a photocopier).
4   E-bay and all such similar hunting, buying and selling facilities. Amongst all else, these enable you to buy information cheaply if you need to.

5   The net is enormous *fun*. Computers and the net enable any number of serious activities and achievements, but they are also wondrous toys. Provided that attribute is not idly indulged, it is a decisively enabling factor for any student: pleasure always is. Indeed, it is likely to keep you working longer if you enjoy using the web rather than the library.

Yet those five and the host of others like them are, finally, *relative*. They might be superior to the old ways and research procedures (which, after all, is what 'progress' is supposed to mean and involve) but they deal with the same needs and desires that have characterised inquisitive minds since the dawn of civilisation.

The democratic nature of the internet is, however, a unique historical phenomenon. Until its instigation, to get anything published meant submitting it to someone, who would then give either the thumbs-up or the thumbs-down.[5] No matter whether the work in question was of earth-shattering significance, worthily important, or abject drivel, the driving criterion was *economics*. In the vast majority of instances, that meant money and only money, ranging from the nervous wish to cover one's costs to the publishing-world Eldorado of a global best-seller. Occasionally, the economic concern was more to do with actually staying alive rather than making money – i.e. publishing something that would enrage and therefore make one a target.[6] But whatever the precise nature of those economics, one fact was constant for all authors, whether would-be, quietly established or hugely successful:

Somebody other than you had to say 'Yes'.

No longer so. Anybody can set up a website; that same anybody can, therefore, – barring certain legal constraints[7] – publish on it anything s/he wants to.

And that is wonderful. It means that the 'ordinary person' has been *truly* empowered, not condescendingly pandered to by such cheap (in both senses) pretences as the phone-in programme, the email response to newspaper articles, media websites and the like. Those are all variants on 'Letters to *The Times*', which may briefly gratify the published writer but beyond that do little or no significant *work*. The internet is in its infancy, but as it develops into adolescence and then maturity, the possibilities for all our voices to be truly heard are excitingly increased.

If that last paragraph strikes you as suspiciously romantic, I have to say that I agree with you. For my second observation is of course . . .

The *worst* thing about the net is that it is democratic

If absolutely anyone can publish stuff on the net, then it is inevitable that the medium will contain more than its fair share of rubbish. I'm not talking about the many, varied and repellent nastinesses that can (all too easily) be accessed; I'm talking about

stuff that may be 'innocent' but is simply *no good*.

In Chapter 2 I argued that plagiarism is not just a vice but enormously dangerous to any student. But even if your net-searching motives are as pure as could be, your judgement must from start to finish be in charge. So when zapping websites, you need to bear in mind these criteria in terms of the material's reliability and/or whether you trust it:

1   Who wrote it? Have you heard of the author? If not, are you able to find out about him/her? The search engines will quickly assist that quest; other productive checking sources include reference books, libraries and your teachers.
2   Does the text make sense to you? Is it plausible?
3   Is it balanced, or pursuing an obvious 'line' or evident bias?
4   How well is it written? Are the mechanics accurate? If not, be immediately suspicious: you will, I hope, recall my earlier observation that a writer who can't be bothered to take care of the little things is invariably no less indifferent to and sloppy about the big ones.
5   Even if the text is flawlessly correct, how do you respond to its style and tone? If it displeases or troubles you, be as suspicious as you should be concerning point 4 above.
6   How does it fit in with what you know already? If it doesn't, are these new ideas exciting and revelatory, or do they seem dodgy?
7   What is the website's purpose? Is it truly educational, or is it trying to sell you something, either literally or metaphorically? Either way, be very wary of such mercenary 'pitches'.
8   To expand point 1: can you cross-reference the text with other authorities and material, so as to confirm or negate its reliability?

And finally:

9   Be wary of Wikipedia, making sure to find another source that corroborates the entry you've consulted. The website in question may not quite be awash with errors, but it has too many mistakes and imprecisions for comfort or safety.

Naturally, all those questions and your responses to them should also characterise your research in other media. But since the net is very likely to be your main source, you should approach it with caution as well as justified enthusiasm. It is still excitingly new, it has immense charm and seemingly awesome potency – and those properties can disarm you in a fashion not entirely dissimilar from the way in which a cobra mesmerises its prey. That's why I used the phrase 'deadly serious' just now: trusting the net *regardless* will not, of course, kill you, but it could kill off your chances of success.

One last piece of advice. If you are writing an assignment of any kind, or even if you're making detailed notes on Word documents and the like, try if possible to

get away from the net, email and every other 'extra' PC facility.

While writing these pages, I found myself regularly breaking off to check emails or visiting my net 'Favourites'. Okay, perhaps I was getting tired or just running low on energy, but it was still not a very bright way to take care of business. Try not to be as dumb as me! If that assignment, draft essay or preliminary note-taking is important to you, tear yourself away – even if it's only a matter of a few feet – from the PC and use a laptop or palm computer or other device that is not connected to the internet; if none is available to you, you'll just have to find more will-power than I have usually been able to exert. In bygone times, writers used to work in a room where there was no phone and, better still, no chance of hearing it elsewhere in the house when it rang. Ignoring the blandishments of the MSN Messenger, the internet and email housed in the machine you're currently using to write is considerably more difficult, but if you want to pass (or, I hope, prosper at) those weak subjects, you will need at times to find a way to do it.

Once again, you might think the connection between this section and being 'a happy student' is a somewhat tenuous one. But if and when you get into a position where the internet is a marvellously enabling source that you fully understand and can intellectually control, you will indeed be happy, satisfied and deeply pleased.

YOUR KEY AUDIENCE: WHO ARE YOU WRITING FOR?

In Chapter 2, I observed – perhaps sternly – that whatever your level and whatever the subject in question, sooner or later you have to realise that the work you're doing is *yours*, nobody else's. Finally, you're not doing this stuff for the teacher, the examiner, your parents, or whomever: you're doing it for *you*.

That does not mean that you should tackle your assignments in a kind of vacuum; you are writing to be *read*, and that requires you to have a sharp sense of your audience.

In an immediate sense, perhaps, that audience *is* your teacher or the examiner. But as I've also observed, it is a great mistake to imagine that you've got to tailor your work to the known or supposed tastes of who will assess your work. Yes, there are a few teachers who want their own views cloned by every pupil, but such instructors are no good, won't last long and in any case are fighting a doomed cause. No decent (or re-hired) examiner has such a mindset: those who formally assess you are interested in whether you know what you're doing and what you're talking about, not whether they agree. Of course, they will penalise you if you commit fundamental inaccuracies, but such basic errors occur far less often – in *all* subjects – than you might think.[8] Beyond the rudimentary level, academic work is a matter of interpretation, of slant, of different ways of seeing and doing things; it is rarely a matter of 'right' and 'wrong'.

Nevertheless – and this is a strategic idea I've learnt only quite recently, thanks to two dear fellow-writer friends – there is a very valuable triple-focus you can activate when writing an assignment, a memo or report, even a business letter. You should have three specific 'reader types' in mind, simultaneously and at all times:

1   You.
2   A close friend who admires and believes in you, and because of that won't want you to get away with anything sloppy or not as good as it might be.
3   A reader who wants you to fail, who for whatever reason will be eager to pick holes in your work. Such a person may be an enemy, someone jealous of you, or merely the kind of mean spirit who, finding excellence a living provocation, is anxious to find as many flaws as possible. It doesn't matter if those are ridiculously trivial: such folk are looking for the 'Gotcha!' moment, and they will do so hard and relentlessly.

Point 1 need take very little explanatory time. Whatever you're doing, if the resultant work doesn't please (or at least satisfy) *you*, the chances of it impressing anyone else are slim.

Point 2: if you know such a person, bind him/her to you with hoops of steel; if not, find one *prontissimo*. Close friends are your best critics, especially if they are bright (and if they're *your* friends, they will be so: I don't write books for dummies!). They will give you praise, which everyone needs; they will quibble and be pedantic – 'Can't you state this more elegantly?', 'What are you driving at here?', 'What is this supposed, actually, to *mean*?' – everyone needs that too. And on occasion they will gently but firmly suggest that you've gone off the rails here, have made an unwise assertion or interpretation there, should perhaps elbow an entire paragraph or section because it isn't good enough.

You might not agree with such advice and comment, and that of course is your privilege and right: sometimes one has to 'go for wotcha know' regardless. But just considering such loving response will almost certainly make your outcome better, even if you act on it in piecemeal rather than comprehensive fashion.

Point 3 may sound paranoid on my part, but it isn't.[9] Many people are generous and excited when they encounter work of quality: because they are themselves very good at what they do and deeply interested in the field in question, impressive things impress them, not least because it broadens and deepens their own knowledge. But there is, sad to say, a plentiful number of other souls who resent talent in others, especially if that talent follows a different line from theirs or proposes a theory that challenges their own.

So towards the end of composing whatever you're engaged upon, try to read it as if you hated yourself, or at least wanted to put yourself down, publicly and gleefully. Such masochism is hard to mobilise, I grant you; but if you scrutinise what you've done with the aim of making it 'bastard-proof', I assure you that you will soon find things you can shore up more solidly, sentences you can make more telling, proofs that are more elegant and illuminating, translations that are both more precise and lucid.

If you satisfy all three readers, you'll have done a first-class job. And that should make you a *very* happy student.

'SWOT' ANALYSIS

The acronym 'SWOT' acquired almost universal currency in the 1990s; it may have become a bit stale now, but it's still useful. It signifies:

S   Strengths
W   Weaknesses
O   Opportunities
T   Threats

The 'happy student' can toughly mobilise that formula to advantage. I'm not just talking about an overall self-appraisal: that's valuable and mature, and will serve you well as you go through life. More specifically and locally, I'm talking about those weak subject areas which trouble you and which, presumably, impelled you to read this book.

Listing your *strengths* ought to be easy enough, but often it surprisingly isn't. In my overwhelming experience, students tend to under- rather than overrate themselves: sometimes they will persist in thinking there are awful at x or y when in fact they are really quite good. So, within reason, be vain! Pat yourself on the back for those things you know you do well or at least competently, and list all of them as strengths.

In view of the probable humility I've just ascribed to you, you should find listing your *weaknesses* less tricky. But don't overdo it: be honest, but not masochistic! Just as you may under-assess your strengths, you can easily exaggerate your fragility.

Your list should include not only academic areas in which you feel less than strong, but habits and routines (or lack of them) which you know mar your study performance. As, for example:

- not meeting deadlines;
- working when you're far from your freshest or best;
- spending too long 'getting ready' to work;
- failing to look over past work regularly enough;
- over-skimpy note-taking;
- thinking in compartmentalised 'subject boxes',

and so on. Just listing them like that will bring them into the forefront of your mind, and that means you've already started to reduce their weakness – you're 'targeting' them.

At a simple level, *opportunities* means making the best and fullest use of your (considerable) gifts. But it also involves thinking more widely. That play you're studying: is there a production of it anywhere? If so, go to see it. That Geography project on climate change: anything on television or radio that might further your knowledge? (At present, that is a strong likelihood.) That Chemistry research you're having trouble with: would a half-term visit to the Science Museum help? Once you start 'thinking outside' the classroom and your desk area, it is remarkable how much you can do – and most enjoyably – to increase your command and interest.

Opportunities also, I firmly believe, should be taken wherever you can. Everyone and virtually everything has got something to teach you: sometimes you'll be as delighted as surprised at what you learn from apparently the most unlikely source. In addition, such avid open-mindedness will automatically lead to an increase in your awareness and expectation of pleasure in what you're undertaking.

Finally, *threats.* I suppose you can list 'exams' under that heading, though by now I hope you feel sufficiently confident about your prospects not to do so. You might also want to include anything that truly troubles you – an unsympathetic teacher, maybe, or becoming so tired and 'stressed out' that both efficiency and pleasure threaten to vanish. However, I trust your list will not be a long one; it might even be that it's blank. I guess I would say this, wouldn't I, but if you've followed the advice and ideas laid out in this book, such blankness is a real possibility.

SWOT is also a valuable tool when composing your CV and/or completing your UCAS form, which is the focus of the next and final chapter.

TROUBLESHOOTING BLOCKAGES

Memory block

Virtually all of us have things that we cannot remember, or find very difficult to do so. For example:

> Some very good drivers who have otherwise extremely retentive minds could not possibly think of being a London cabbie, simply because they're hopeless at remembering even the street names in their own neighbourhood, let alone those of the entire London A–Z that comprise what cabbies fondly, and with justifiable pride, call 'The Knowledge'.

It seems to make no difference how hard these people try, or how often they're embarrassed by and about it (and no one likes looking an idiot) – it just won't happen for them. Is there nothing you can do about such 'memory blind spots'? Are they insoluble?

No, they're not. The first step is to admit 'I'm blocked' and accept the situation rather than worry at it. That might not make you happy, but it will allow you to relax and acquire initial control. Then see if you can unblock things via mnemonics, looking at the material from a different angle and the various other techniques collected in Chapter 3, 'Top tips'. If none of those brings any improvement, try one or other of the following.

1   Recite the information to be learned onto a tape, then play it back as often as you can stand. Once you've got over the usual ghastliness of hearing your voice as it sounds to others, it may be that the fact that it *is* your voice will render the material more immediate and learner-friendly.

2   Try to establish (or manufacture) connections between the things to be learnt. It is invariably easier to remember material that is 'grouped' rather than single.

3   Divide the material into smaller sections – single items if need be (point 2 notwithstanding) – and work on them fiercely but briefly. Return to them as often as you can bear: it won't be pleasant, but you might get a result!

4   Write it out for yourself in note form. The act of writing engages more of the brain than just reading, and – analogous to the voice point in number 1 above – the sight of the information in your own hand rather than impersonal typescript might help.

If none of those succeeds, there are just two things left:

5   Hope that the block will one day simply clear itself, as it were of its own volition.

6   See what sheer stinking vanity will do!

Point 6 is less facetious than you might think. A surprising amount of excellent work is fuelled by either vanity or rage – or indeed both. If you decide you're determined not to let this stuff get the better of you, the chances are better than even that it won't. And that should make you happy; at the very least, a kind of grim satisfaction should ensue.

Learning blocks

These are different from memory blocks in that they have to do with *attitudes* and *organisation* rather than neurological failure. They come about through diffidence, dislike or sheer prejudice – the kind of knee-jerk reaction to a subject or topic that Ian Sheldon so skilfully exposed as not only unwise but quite unnecessary.[10] I hope that the top tips Ian and others provide in Chapter 3 will have brought about the removal of most such blockages, but it is possible that you may still be residually resistant to certain areas of your work.

If that problem concerns classwork or any kind of public learning session, I have urged you to take what you can out of that time however unsympathetic the teacher or the environment. Private work on uncongenial tasks is another matter, and arguably both trickier and potentially more damaging. The analogy which follows will I hope assist you.

I would be very surprised if this hasn't happened to you. You've been invited to a meal in somebody's home, and when the main course arrives, you quickly realise that it's a mixture of things you like very much, some you're perfectly okay with, and an item or two that you don't fancy one little bit. Assuming that you are the courteous and gracious person I imagine, you are constrained; very anxious to seem pleased; chiefly, though, wondering how on earth you're going to disguise your dislike of those offending items.[11] And you probably decide to get them out of the way at once, washed down with a refreshing drink. The ordeal is soon over, and your hostess will be pleased to think you tucked into those foods with such gusto – a sizeable Brownie-points fringe benefit, that, however unfounded! Then, relaxed and relieved, you start in on the rest of the plate, and if you're anything like me, you'll save your favourite items till the end. Job done; everyone happy – especially you.

Adopt the same principle when working at your desk. Let us assume you are going to do about two hours' work on three separate tasks that must, or at any rate *should*, be completed that evening. As with that problematic meal:

1   Start with the 'worst'/least congenial/most resistant one. Pick a topic with a view to getting somewhere with it – not mastery, but progress. Limit to 15–20 minutes.
2   Go on to the second item, but not your 'favourite' yet . . .
3   Keep that 'plum' as the third task, about forty-five minutes in to the session. Have a good break first, then climb in and enjoy!
4   By then you should feel properly pleased with yourself. Use that 'feel-good factor' and earned strength: go back to point 1 and consolidate/confirm progress. That will make you feel even better.

Once you get into that rhythm, it's remarkable how quickly it can become a permanent and enabling feature. It will even see you through times when other factors have combined to make you depressed or worried: there's nothing like a really productive work session to convince you that, all the way round, things are pretty okay, really.

I suffer from 'blocks' myself; however, without being self-lacerating – or by extension a pompous pulpit-basher – those 'can't do it' items are finally a matter of laziness rather than incompetence. They are *excuses*, not *reasons*, further examples of the damaging attitudes examined at the start of Chapter 2. As a Frenchman once said:

> *Si tu veux, tu peux.*

'If you want to, you can'. Yes indeed. You can unblock things if you really *care* about doing so, and nothing breeds study happiness more than turning what was a blocked sink into a place where you're suddenly able to swim.

CONCLUSION

It strikes me that this chapter's title could seem rather simplistic in the light of what I've then gone on to advise and observe, much of which is *tough*. Obviously, though, I stick to it. Happy is, in fact, a very big word so far as I'm concerned: it weighs in just below *joy* in my emotional hierarchy, and is therefore not something I expect to be a permanent feature of my life. Maybe I should have cited *contentment* instead. But no matter, really, whatever *le mot juste*. If you get your life and work (and your loves, too!) in order, there is virtually no end to the ways in which you can advance, conquer and become fully in charge.

As – and before – we move to the final chapter about how you can persuade the world beyond that you are indeed in charge and worth investing in, I would like to draw your attention to Appendix I, which addresses Poetry Commentary. It can, I trust, be usefully read even by those of you who do not and/or never again will study literature: in keeping with the top tips core of this book, that appendix crosses all boundaries in its focus on the specifics that underscore *any* subject/discipline.

Chapter 7

Balancing it

The virtues of failure

Success lies not only in the destination but in your experiences along the way.

Robin Sieger

Once a philosopher, twice a pervert.

Voltaire

The 'orthodox' CV: introduction

'CV' signifies 'Curriculum Vitae'. Many Latin phrases which have passed into mainstream English are welcome and valuable imports, but I've been never been too keen on this one: it is both pompous and, worse, imprecise. It roughly translates as 'the history of (one's) life', but such telegraphed comprehensiveness does not begin to characterise the orthodox CV, which is a record of achievements, posts held, things done. Those things are of course important, but they hardly add up to a full account of a life, whether one is sixty or sixteen. However crucial to one's future, the CV is a limited record of the past; the 'history' it documents is an entirely external matter, and in no sense does it resemble a mini-biography. Moreover,

almost invariably, the CV is a record of *successful* outcomes only

which means that in effect and to all intents and purposes:

it is a selling document, and the product is *you*.

And therein lies a very large problem for almost all students when they tackle their UCAS application. To help solve that, I want to look at the whole process in a way that might be unorthodox but will, I am confident, prove beneficial.

I have yet to meet a sixth former who does not find his/her UCAS application an ordeal, or at the very least something that causes immense difficulty and takes a very long time to get right. There are a number of reasons for that, and they deserve detailed consideration:

1   Form-filling is always intimidating.

2   Only those (very rare) souls who find swanking an uncomplicated pleasure feel comfortable about composing what is, in effect, or at least appears so, an orgy of trumpet-blowing.

3   As noted already, the CV/UCAS application mainly logs one's *past*. And while that record may be gratifying and quietly pride-inducing, it seems to have little to do with what one is doing *now*.

4   Whoever and wherever you are, you get a mass of conflicting advice. Different teachers tell you different things; parents, friends and siblings weigh in; after a few weeks, you feel you know *less*, not more.

5   Because your school/institution is itself under fierce pressure to deliver the entire UCAS application on time, you are pressured to 'complete' before you feel ready.

6   Some young people know what they want to do, where they want to do it, so forth, even before they enter the Sixth Form. But not many; after all, most of you are being asked to make serious and semi-binding career decisions before the end of your second term in the Sixth Form. In my view that is poisonously ludicrous, but since we're all stuck with it, the more important point is that you must not be bullied into making a choice for the sake of it/the institution's convenience. That is easily said on my part; it is desperately difficult to do on yours.

7   'How do I know what I think till I see what I say?' That wonderful observation was made by the novelist E.M. Forster, and it applies to UCAS forms as much as it does to any sixth-form 'exploratory' assignment (i.e. learning experience rather than performance art). Especially in view of point 1 above, you can't do a proper job until you feel truly comfortable about what you are tackling.

And, of course, finally:

8   How on earth do I *start*?!

Let us dwell – I hope fruitfully – on those eight points in turn, and then look at ways in which you can counter/deal with/surmount the problems that they pose.

1   Whoever you are, however young or old, whatever the matter in question might be, an official form is at best problematic and at worst nadgeringly unnerving. I am now into my seventh decade on this planet, and form-filling still bothers me. Especially my annual tax return: it troubles me every time – and I'm not a crook or seeking to pull fast ones! And if I feel like that – as do many others of the same vintage – what kind of effect does it have on a person not yet twenty years old? At times, I think, UCAS-advising teachers are not sufficiently aware of that factor; I believe I am, and that what follows will truly assist you.

2   Literally two weeks before writing these words, I asked an Upper Sixth set (highly talented, full of promise) why they encountered problems writing a Personal Statement when their writing elsewhere – essays, letters, reports – was so skilful, classy and at ease. Several students said, at once: 'I find it so difficult to persuade some unknown bureaucrat that I'm worth bothering with, let alone good. So many other people I know seem better.' A charming reaction; also an utterly natural one. But it 'freezes' you.

3   It is hard to get excited about one's past achievements. Satisfied and quite proud, yes; excited, no. You are writing this application because of what you've achieved, but there is an almost spooky disparity between that *past*, what you're (nervously, in the best sense) doing *now*, and what you envisage doing *later*. And that means you find it very hard to write coherently, even grammatically, when UCAS form-filling.

4   UCAS procedures have changed a good deal in the last five years, and nowhere more so than the Personal Statement. A significant number of teachers/tutors haven't truly digested this, and thus give well-meaning but precariously outdated advice. Box 10, as the Personal Statement is officially designated, is now primarily an academic manifesto, outlining in detail why you want to study the subject you've chosen and why you want to do it at the universities you've cited. Your hobbies and school record are not unimportant, but they are decidedly secondary.

5 & 6   As noted, in my private view it is quite insane that students not yet six months into their Sixth Form courses are pressured to decide

'what they want to do' two years hence and beyond. But we are all imprisoned in this grim farce until some decisively wise and powerful government does something about it. All I can say, given the pressure your institution undoubtedly will exert, is that you try to relax and don't give in: wait till you're ready. The truth is that you don't have to submit until mid-December, and teachers who press you for an answer in the preceding April are being neither fair nor realistic.

7   The uniquely fraught business of *writing* the Personal Statement deserves a whole section to itself, including the almost poisonously vexed question . . .

8   . . . How to start? The quick answer to that is 'in the middle' – address the filling first, and deal with the sandwich bread later. That promised section follows shortly. First, though, I want briefly to consider how valuable *mistakes* and *failure* can be.

Enabling alternatives 1: the 'anti-CV'

We have established that composing a CV is a difficult, even alien experience precisely because it logs only one's *past*. And it is a curious fact that our successes come to matter to us much less than we thought they would when we were striving for them. Once a student has accomplished a goal, it might be overstating the case to suggest that his/her attitude becomes

been there, done that, got the T-shirt,

but the impulse is to move on, to find new things to do, new fields to explore and conquer.

There's an even more significant aspect to this phenomenon. By and large I would say that, looked at in the medium or long term, success is good for people and failure isn't. All of us are fragile however strong we might appear on the surface, and nothing aids confidence and proper self-esteem more than to have some successes under your belt, to feel that you are good at what you do and in charge of it. Such confidence can also make you nicer, more generous: if you like yourself, it's easier to be kind to others, to be good and enabling company. Conversely, failure can easily lead one to become first withdrawn and then aggressively defensive or touchy, and eventually 'bitter and twisted', as the phrase has it. Moreover, people who feel they are failures are often not very honest about it: they blame everything other than themselves, which I'm afraid renders them extremely boring as well as stuck in a sterile rut.

However, and paradoxically:

> We learn from our failures, mistakes and hideous screw-ups *much more* than we do from our successes.

And that means that you should almost *treasure* your failures, or at least acknowledge them with humour and clear-sightedness.

So: make out a list of the things you've fluffed recently. I don't want to turn you into a craven masochist, so keep it short for the time being! They can be to do with academic work, with sport, with social relationships, anything. I am a great admirer of the now almost-forgotten American comedian Shelly Berman, who prefaced one of his routines with a beautifully honest and humble admission with which I very much identify – and I'm sure I'm not alone in that:

> Do you have moments in your life which you look back on and say, 'AAAAARRRRRGGGGHHHH!! Why did I do it? *Why did I do it?'* Well, I have *thousands* of them.

To get you going, here are a few such buttock-clenchingly awful experiences that have either happened to me or which I've imagined (and no, I'm not going to identify which is which!). They will I hope amuse, but as I hope is clear enough by now, there is a deeply serious intent underlying them also.

So, as said: make out a list – *now* – of things you've messed up, things that have excruciatingly embarrassed you, things that you never, ever want to repeat. Then do two things:

1 Laugh! They *are* funny, aren't they? You'd laugh yourself sick if they happened to anyone else – even a loved friend. Why not do the same for yourself?
2 Write down what you've learnt from those ghastly moments, and *why* you will never, ever want to repeat them.

Then do two other things, concentrating this time solely on study/work matters.

3 Write down a recent academic experience that was less than satis-factory. It could be a lousy lesson; a piece of work you did not do

What I did	Why I shouldn't have	What have I learnt?
Texted my girlfriend all evening	I had a History essay due for submission next morning	1 I love texting my girlfriend. 2 Last-night deadlines are always bad news: avoid that by earlier completion – then be free to enjoy texting, serenely and even smugly!
Got drunk	Should've drunk tea or milk instead	1 Tea is a very dull drink. 2 Milk is so much less tasty now thanks to EU obsessionalism. 3 Getting drunk is nice but . . . 4 . . . The aftermath is horrible, and wastes a lot of time.
Was foul-mouthed and additionally horrible to my girlfriend	No answer required!	1 Bought her flowers and . . . 2 . . . Women receiving flowers after a spat either think men are feeling guilty or that they (the women, that is) now have the power. So: 3 Don't be foul-mouthed and horrible again, for several vital reasons.
Flirted with a prattish man to make my boyfriend jealous	It always backfires	Honesty is the best policy – not so much morally as allowing you to feel clean and good about yourself.
Turn off from Chemistry because the teacher is both dull and aggressive	I'm the only loser – he gets paid regardless; I've got an academic career to build	Take it where you can: everyone's got something to give you, provided you let yourself receive it.
Fart explosively at a formal dinner party	Obvious; but when an outraged husband said, 'How dare you fart before my wife?', I really shouldn't have said, 'I'm so sorry! – I didn't realise it was her turn.'	1 Nobody loves a smart-alec. 2 Cut down on the red wine and the baked beans. 3 Don't go to lousy dinner parties: life's too short.

well; a piece of work you thought was misunderstood/not marked
fairly; something you didn't understand and failed to say so; virtually
anything.

4   Then consider – and preferably write down again – what you think
you might have *learnt* from such failure. How might you respond
positively to such times in the future? Have you learnt not to make
the same mistake again? Are those that misunderstood your work
or whose teaching you do not entirely follow aware of that? Can
you talk to them?

With that last in mind, a personal anecdote about something that
occurred while I was actually writing this chapter.

This year (2007–8) I am teaching Milton and Romanticism to a quite
outstanding Upper Sixth set. With one exception, their first (large)
Milton assignment was sparklingly good – substantial, stylish, penetrating
and full of insight, authority and pleasure. The one exception was a
very able boy whose written expression was markedly inferior to his
intellect: his sentences rambled, he was Scrooge-like in punctuation and
all those things that help the reader grasp what you want to say. I drew
his attention to that in my comments at the end, and (of course) made
no public reference to the fact that he was at present 'the odd one out'.

Less than twenty-four hours later I received this email from him:

> Would it be possible in this up-coming week for us to talk about
> essay writing, please? I wouldn't put this to you if I wasn't fairly
> worried about January's exams and how my technique is and has
> been found lacking in exams and practice essays.

I wrote back (in part):

> Of course. I greatly admire you for such a prompt and humble res-
> ponse. You're an able guy, and between us we can sort it, I'm sure.

And we did. But the point is that he had to *ask*, he had to *do* something
about it – take an initiative, learn from his shortcomings and actively
respond. I can't quite believe I'm about to write these next words, but
there's an old Jewish proverb which runs:

> Success makes you clever; problems make you wise.

Absolutely. Admitting you have problems, looking at them full-on, and
cheerfully recognising that there are benefits to be had from the bad

times as well as from the good are the keys to real, lasting success. And take comfort also from Voltaire's remark that heads this chapter:

> Once a philosopher, twice a pervert.

That brilliantly witty observation means that it is perfectly all right to make a mistake – even a bad one – *once*: indeed, such an error, if properly reflected on, should make you wiser and more enabled. The thing to avoid is making the same mistake twice: chronic error is perverse, not least because it shows that the perpetrator is not learning, not even thinking.

Enabling alternatives 2: the virtues of the third person

Normally, to refer to yourself in the third person is a singularly unattractive attribute: it signals either immense arrogance or idiocy. One of the things that marks out Julius Caesar's dangerous (to both himself and Rome) aloofness in Shakespeare's play that bears his name is his regular habit of using 'Caesar' instead of 'I', always in a fashion that suggests he is inordinately pleased with himself and considers himself above all other folk. Actors and other celebrities adopt such a pose from time to time, invariably to their detriment; and professional boxers have, increasingly, developed the habit of using their full names when discussing a bout or their training, and it always sounds ridiculous – an unedifying mixture of the pompous and the cretinous.

Nevertheless, the practice can be both unexceptionable and useful in certain circumstances, and nowhere more so, I suggest, than when starting to compile a CV or Personal Statement. I've already observed that the majority of young people (and many older ones too) feel constrained when asked to list their achievements, strengths and qualities: very quickly they feel they are indulging a frenzy of self-advertisement on the lines of:

> Hey! I'm really amazing – young, gifted and everything you'd want.

So replace the 'I' with 'He' or 'She'. Write about yourself as if you were a sympathetic, supportive but tough and unblinking referee. You'll soon find that this is a much more comfortable way of logging your achievements and ambitions. If you still feel a bit constrained, use the SWOT pattern addressed in the previous chapter. Keep to the third person still, but itemise weaknesses and threats as well as strengths and opportunities. You won't include the former two in your finished application, but to consider such 'negatives' along the way is itself a strength, and can also make you more sharply aware of what your assets are.

That is *how* you might start. Now let's return to *where* you might do so. Returning to the sandwich metaphor I used earlier, fix your attention on the filling, on the central substance. That means:

1 What subject you wish to study;
2 *Why* you want to study it;
3 (*Where* you want to study it.)

I've put the third in brackets not because it's less important but because it almost certainly will only come into play once you're clear about the other two.

Number 2 is both crucial and decidedly problematic. You have got to be ruthless with yourself – and possibly others – about this. University application is an intensely competitive business, and if you come across as not fully locked-on to your proposed course of study, literate in and about it, and doing it for all the right reasons, you are likely to be by-passed. All the impressive past exam grades in the world will not do you much good if your application smacks of the dilettante or the half-hearted.

Be especially careful about 'careerist' reasons – and here you might face battles (or at any rate some awkward moments) with parents. In some disciplines, of course – medicine and veterinary science come most obviously to mind – the eventual career is automatically predicated on the course of study; such cases are in a minority, however. You don't need to read English to be a journalist or Media Studies to work in radio and television; you don't need to read Economics or Business Studies to become an accountant; you don't need to read Theology to become a priest, and so forth.

That is not to say that such degree–profession connections don't exist: of course they do. But the real point I'm driving at is that you should

> do the degree subject you find most congenial and attractive, *regardless of other considerations.*

That might appear to be slightly romantic or over-indulgent advice; on the contrary, it is toughly and profoundly realistic, for two reasons.

1 *You stand a much better chance of securing a good or excellent degree if you really* like *what you're doing.* Firms employ graduates for their potential, not for what they've done. The days are long gone when graduates were hired because of what they *knew*; twenty-first-century graduates, however erudite and wide-ranging their accomplishments, know only a small proportion of what their subject entails. They are not experts; there may even be areas of their discipline in which they are barely literate. That is emphatically not to denigrate today's young, whom I much admire and believe in: it is, instead, a recognition that the information explosion of the last fifty or so years has transformed the 'education template'. Graduates are hired for their intelligence, for their proven ability to absorb information, ideas and material and to re-process it intelligibly and with authority. And they are also hired because they have done very well at what they chose to do: successful graduates know their own worth, their own strengths and interests, their own desires, and people like that are always going to be worth investing in.

The second reason is closely related to the first . . .

2 *Whatever profession you end up choosing as a graduate, you will be trained in that calling from scratch. It will not matter what you've done, only what they confidently believe you can now do.* That is a hugely liberating advantage: it means you can concentrate on each strand at a time – university, possible postgraduate work, then career choice and training – rather than second-guess what you might be wanting to do in six year's time at the age of twenty-four. It also means that you can radically switch focus as a graduate – from History to Law, from Natural Sciences to Engineering, from English or Languages to Advertising, from practically anything to Accountancy (provided your Maths is sound). However, the fact remains that at eighteen years old you're likely to get a lot of quite conflicting advice. Which brings us back to those outside – especially parental – pressures.

There are a lot of cultural-myth jokes about 'Number one son to be doctor/lawyer/whatever', and they don't just centre on the Jewish and the Chinese communities, even if those are perhaps the most commonly cited instances. Every nation has a fair number of parents who are pressingly deterministic about such matters. And those parents are almost invariably *wrong*, even if the outcome turns out to be less than disastrous.

It is *your* life and career: not your parents', not your peers', not your beloved's. There is only one thing worse than marrying someone for the wrong reasons (and there are plenty of those), and that's entering a career for the wrong reasons. After all – and I am not remotely a cynical man – you can always marry again; re-starting a career is rather more difficult, and less propitious.

'They' might want you to be a lawyer; so, actually, might you. But do *you* want to study Law as your *first* degree? If so, you had better enjoy reading – most Law courses require you to read thirty to forty books (or case histories) a week. If you're currently struggling to read one or two books a *month*, maybe you'd better re-think, whatever Daddy, Mummy, Wise Uncle or Knowing Aunt might say. Or 'they' might want you to be a doctor. Is that what *you* want?

During the late 1980s and early 1990s, a colleague and I were responsible for mock-interviewing all our school's Oxbridge candidates (on average, about thirty boys). One year we interviewed a student who was terribly unsuited to the profession he was trying to pursue.

The real – and deeply serious – implication of this was that here was a nice (if rather solemn) and certainly clever young man who had been appallingly badly advised, or rather, dictatorially channelled into a wholly unsuitable career choice. He eventually became a chemical engineer – and, I have subsequently learnt, a good and successful one.

As we come to the end of this modest enquiry into the benefits of failure and mistakes, a word or two about another recent student phenomenon – and complication – is in order.

Enabling alternatives 3: the gap year

I say 'enabling alternative', but that is not entirely so across the board. For a start, as UCAS itself stresses:

1   *If you are looking to read Maths or Physics, a gap year is most unwise.* Good mathematicians and physicists, let alone very good or indeed truly brilliant ones, do their best work by the time they're in their early twenties. It makes absolutely no sense to devote one such prime year to other activities, however admirable, exciting and worthy they may be. To do so will sacrifice momentum, maybe crucially and certainly observably. Don't run that risk.

2   *What do you want to have a gap year for?* Are your reasons truly muscular? One answer to that first question which I hear quite often is:

> I want a break from the education conveyor-belt. I've been doing annual exams for five solid years – Key Stage 3, GCSE, AS and A2 (or IB), and although I've been happy and successful, I don't want an immediate three further years of the same.

I am highly sympathetic to that response; who would not be? The remorseless grind and pressure that students of this generation have to endure are out of all proportion more severe than anything I had to cope with in the 1960s – and my generation had the additional luxury (and benefit) of, commonly, three years in the Sixth Form, not a compacted two.

But it isn't enough to take a year out *just* for that reason. Okay, the gap year might be the one time for the next thirty-plus years where you have a chance to do something genuinely different, imaginative, even life-changing. If that is the case, wonderful: do it. But don't use your gap year as an excuse to get a bit of part-time work, catch up on your reading (ha ha: don't waste my – or, more importantly, *your* –time), or slide into being a semi-couch potato. You're having an invigorating furlough at the age of eighteen/nineteen: you are not *retiring*! I'm being quite serious: talking to some post-gap year students about what they did during that time fills me with depression. It not only emerges that they did little if anything of significance, but their minds have become somehow blunted, possibly jeopardising their undergraduate career before it even starts.

That is, I freely admit, a 'worst possible scenario'; I equally concede that many students grow enormously as minds, burgeoning adults and indeed human beings as a result of their gap year enterprises. All I'll say in summary is this:

> The gap year is an opportunity unique to your generation. By all means seize that opportunity – but in a way that decisively mobilises you. If you fancy a doss, well, okay; but remember that more often than not, dossers are tossers.

The 'orthodox' CV: the business

I hope the preceding four sections have made you more confident about approaching any post-school applications, especially UCAS. You should now be clearer about what is of prime importance, how and why you should go about choosing precisely what you want to do for the next few years, and feel less constrained or embarrassed about selling yourself.

If that last is not quite yet the case, cheer yourself up by remembering that we all have to go through this and do it. As Robert Louis Stevenson tellingly observed:

> Everyone lives by selling something.

How you best do that – so that you avoid cringing as you write *and* come over in a positive, sympathique but suitably professional manner, hinges on something that applies to any and all writing:

> It's vital to get the *tone* as attractive and appropriate as you can.

Following the 'third person strategy' will help a good deal, I believe: it shouldn't be too difficult to transfer the controlled, sober warmth of that initial document into a first-person statement. Among other things it should make sure that you

> don't *gush*.

It is a great mistake to come on strong with such sentences as:

1 I have a passion for history.
2 Since I was a little girl nature has fascinated me deeply.
3 It has long been my goal to be an outstanding pathologist.

All three remarks may very well be true, but they fall uneasily on the ear. You can say almost exactly the same thing in a fashion that does not seem attention-seeking or arch.

4 The study of history has absorbed me for a long time now.
5 The planet on which we live, its countless and beautiful phenomena, and the way it coalesces has been my main interest since I was very young.
6 The study of disease and why people die compels me in its own right and as a means of making future generations more protected and longer-living.

All right, those alternatives are longer and more elaborate than those they replace. But that's exactly the point: 4–6 offer immediate hard and detailed information about why the candidate wishes to do what s/he has chosen, and effects it in a way both fluent and un-self-conscious.

I made up all six of those opening sallies. Here are two authentic examples. Both opening sentences are arresting and specific, which in turn sets up a fluency and focus in what follows. The first was penned by a History candidate:

> By studying History at school, I have learnt that the subject involves far more than simply enjoying the narratives of the past, however pleasurable that may be. More importantly, it is the study of human behaviour and endeavour, and the causation and consequence of actions taken on an individual, local, national or international scale, which fascinate me. I am also attracted by the breadth and diversity on offer and, conversely, the opportunities for specialisation and original research . . .

Just three sentences – but the boy is *in*! Those eighty words show a grasp of what drives our species; the compulsion of the past and the humanity of the dead; a profound desire to learn for its own excellent sake. In short, it betokens a true scholarly mind and – very loudly though elegantly – a seriously able young man. It is devoid of swank, yet full of dignified confidence. Just the sort of person any teacher would want to teach, in fact. I rest my case.

The second exemplar is a medic. She is no less impressive:

> My interest in medicine stems from my long-standing fascination with all aspects of science and my desire to pursue an intellectually stimulating career that offers a wide range of opportunities. I would find the ability to improve other people's quality of life immensely rewarding, and that a career in medicine would enable me to fulfil my potential in that respect. I am attracted by the high level of personal involvement with people as well as the opportunities for medical research . . .

Different discipline, same classiness. Spectacularly unlike the hapless Hong Kong boy dramatised above, this young lady will be a wonderful doctor: she cares very much about people, as all the best scientists do. Indeed, the best definition of the good scientist/technologist that I've encountered is this, coined in a semi-casual conversation by a good friend of mine who is a civil engineer:

> At root, and whatever else, scientists want to help people have a better and happier time.

That's what I try to do as an English teacher and writer; it should surprise nobody that precisely the same motivation impels those who do science. If you doubt that, check out those 'top tips' in Chapter 3: all disciplines, and all good teachers/practitioners, are remarkably alike in both their methods and their ultimate goals and motivation.

Like her History counterpart, this young lady was in by the time the Admissions Tutor had read those first three sentences. She has an unfeigned and profound desire to serve; she is also toughly interested in the rigorous disciplines medicine embraces. A fairly hefty combination, and one that any sentient university would jump at. And as a kind of 'PS' before we move on to the finale of this chapter and indeed this book: it should not surprise you, I hope, to learn that both candidates were accepted by their first choice universities – which were, respectively, Oxford and Cambridge.

The jury is still out on the vices and virtues of the Personal Statement – not just in UCAS terms but its continued impingement on all modes of career application. The 'pro' lobby would say something along these lines, I guess:

> The Personal Statement is evidence of your ability to be succinct and decisively self-aware. It 'speaks' directly to the reader in a way that mere statistical information cannot do, and thus offers a valuable early clue to your personality.

The opposing lobby might counter with:

> The Personal Statement is invariably smug at best and a kind of lexical masturbation at worst. It is unpleasantly pre-emptive in 'laying the truth' on the reader before s/he has even started to get to know the person; it also pre-empts the process of discovery which is the core of the *interview*, and is therefore impertinent – in both senses – on a CV.

One final example. What do you make of the (authentic) CV reproduced on the facing page, including the Personal Statement?

I hope you would agree that it is clearly and professionally laid out, and it is easy to find the information needed. However, consider the number of times that 'I' appears in the Personal Statement: a mistake, I think, doing nothing to dispel the problem of egotistical overdrive! In addition, if I were to be brutal, it has a 'Blue Peter' feel to it – all a bit squeaky clean and determinedly *nice*. I am convinced that this was

Name	Caroline Margaret HERMAN
Address	42A, Beechwood Drive, Balham, SW12 8TN
Telephone	0181 673 5792
Date of Birth	25 June, 1972
Marital Status	Single; no dependants

A confident communicator, I integrate easily into teams, though I am equally happy to work alone. I am a quick, logical thinker with an analytical mind and enjoy the stimulation of a challenge. I like variety and am adaptable in different situations, to which I respond with enthusiasm and a sense of humour. I am computer-literate and am always keen to learn something new.

QUALIFICATIONS

July 1995	BA (Hons) in French and Linguistic Science; Class II Division I
June 1990	'A' Levels in Mathematics (A), Latin (A) and French (B); 'AS' Level in French (Merit)
June 1998	10 GCSEs in English Language, English Literature, French, Latin, Art, Mathematics, Physics, Biology, Chemistry and Religious Education

EDUCATION

Oct 91–July 95	University of Reading (University of Tours, France 93/4)
Sept 90–July 91	Private Dance Course
Sept 86–July 90	Norwich High School

not Caroline Herman's fault: – such an unfortunate effect was then virtually endemic to the Personal Statement format itself. And the worst thing about all this is – to revisit a point made above about why one should never 'gush' – it didn't really matter if everything logged is *true*, as it was in this case. It still didn't read quite right.

I hope this chapter has enabled you to be confident that, if you follow the advice I've given and are wary of the snares I've identified, your application will very much read right. As with all I've been concerned with in this book, really, it boils down to a combination of tough humility, clear-sighted awareness of how your frailties can be quietly turned into strengths, and of being personally in charge.

I never say 'good luck' to my students before an exam. 'Luck' has nothing to do with it. I wish them joy, or at least enjoyment, of the opportunity to prove how good they are. I wish you the same.

Appendix I
Poetry commentary

Before reading this appendix, you might find it useful to peruse the English 'top tips' offered by Andrew Speedy Esq. in Chapter 3. All of his advice underscores what now follows.

Form and/'versus' content

First and foremost: no decent poet, let alone a great one, makes a regular habit of *deciding on form and metre first*. There might, yes, be times when they do so, as an exercise or 'challenge', and nearly all poets will on occasion choose the sonnet form. But in the main and almost invariably, the poet's initial thoughts and 'launch' will centre on:

> What do I want to say? What 'voice' do I want to say it in? And how much have I got to say – how long does the poem need to be?

You will note that the question of length/substance crops up there; however, the real emphasis is on *content*. Once the writer has a clear idea of that, *then* (but only then) s/he will set about finding the optimum form and structure.

Breaking off from that governing argument to consider a few technical terms, let's start with *iambic pentameters*. An *iambus* is a two-syllabled 'foot' consisting of one short and then one long syllable. *Pentameter* simply means a line with five such feet – ten syllables in all. It is the classic form of blank verse, and I would guess that eighty per cent at least of Shakespeare's work uses it; here is a renowned example – the opening line of *Twelfth Night*. Notice that the stress is always on the even-numbered syllable:

If music be the food of love, play on . . .

The iambic pentameter has also proved timelessly popular, used by many writers to this day (and beyond, I have no doubt). The reason for this is very simple: the line is the closest approximation there is to the natural rhythms of everyday speech. Shakespeare's words may be fearsomely difficult at times, but he communicates easily despite that sophistication because one can 'hear' him naturally and with pleasure.

So, if a poet wants to 'speak' in a natural, intimate voice, s/he may well at least consider that form, or a variant of it. If, on the other hand, s/he wants something more formal – a tone that is akin to a sermon, a declamation or whatever – then another form, less natural and more rigid, might be appropriate. Always remember that,

in the last analysis, form *serves* content.

In a truly great poem, the two become almost indivisible, and one matches, strengthens and dramatises the other.[1] Whatever the quality or format, though, exquisite form will not compensate for stale or inadequate *matter*. To amplify and clarify what that means in terms of how you should best approach critical commentary, I want to examine two essentially opposing stances taken up by two great but very different poets.

In his *Essay on Criticism* (1711), Alexander Pope wrote:

True Art is Nature to advantage dress'd;
What oft was thought, but ne'er so well express'd.

I'm not sure I can agree; or to put it another way, it strikes me that Pope's definition is highly precarious as a working model for anyone less gifted than he. What it can too easily lead to is something stylish, witty, elegant and all the rest of it – but which really doesn't *say* very much.

In almost total contrast, T.S. Eliot observed:

A poem should give you something to think about. When I read a poem and understand it first time, then I know it isn't much good.

Of the two, I consider Eliot's the sounder maxim – especially for students engaged on literary analysis. If you find that all you end up doing is talking about alliteration, line length, neat turns of phrase and an ordered rhyme scheme without happening upon anything to say about what the poem *does* to you, you can't possibly be engaged. Matters of technique and craft are, it is true, absorbing and satisfying – but only if those things serve some other higher and deeper purpose. If there is no evidence that such purpose exists, the poem is by definition shallow, a mere exercise. And to zoom in on your needs and concerns as a student, it is very difficult – almost impossible – to write a cogent and profound analysis of something that is irredeemably shallow.

Those baleful last few sentences should not depress or alarm you: they are intended only to sharpen your awareness of what you're looking at and doing, and also instil in you a sense of literary priorities. The good news is that regardless of level, board or organisation, my experience as teacher and examiner is that:

> Inconsequential, shallow or 'mere exercise' texts hardly ever feature in literature exams.

Sometimes (I would say) the set material in question may not be very *good*, but it invariably has enough substance for you to get your teeth into it and show your mettle.

Both to move forward and to sum up: all that means that the student's prime task is to work out *what the poem is about* and what the poet fundamentally *wants to say*. After that has been accomplished, the next thing is to work out *how* s/he does it. If you follow that order of things, the technical considerations will fall much more easily and smoothly into place.

One further and very important initial point:

> Versification and rhyming are not only a way of achieving clarity and precision; they also assert *control*.

The latter can take the form of unremarkable though satisfying order – something any decent (let alone distinguished) work of art requires. But in certain circumstances it becomes more than that. In any poem about madness or distress or obsession (which characterise many First World War poems, for example), the metre, the rhythm and indeed the very fashioning of the words is an attempt to 'tame' the demons and random fizzing thoughts by nailing them down in some kind of coherent pattern.

In extreme cases, it seems to me, this technique amounts to an attempt to 'defeat' the ailment by trapping it in language: if you can do that, you're not yet entirely mad. But sometimes the power of a poem resides in the realisation – speaker's and reader's – that it hasn't worked: at least two First World War poems by Siegfried Sassoon describe that experience, and I'm sure many other examples could be found. Here now are two classic cases that I hope interest you anyway, and are also worth remembering when you address this aspect of poetic composition.

'Porphyria's Lover' by Browning is a poem about a homicidal psychopath who murders his (occasional) upper-class mistress on the basis of doing her an enormous favour, guaranteeing eternal happiness for both of them. The narrative is matter-of-fact – almost like an adult bedtime story! – and the rhyme scheme is metronomically ordered: a, b, a, b, b; c, d, c, d, d; and so on. Indeed, the whole poem is a minor masterpiece of measured order, narrative logic and clear thinking – *and it is articulated by a speaker who is utterly barking mad!* That's an example of form assisting content by being in absolute contrast to it: a kind of *reverse mimesis.*

The most searing and frequent example, though, is the last work of Sylvia Plath. Philip Larkin wrote a superb essay on her called 'Horror Poet', and he was right on the button. In the last year or so she tried to control the madness she knew was overtaking her in a series of poems addressing her fractured selves and their increasingly vortex-like behaviour.[2] Unfortunately, it did not work – or at any rate it did not save her: she committed suicide a short while after. That fact gives the poems an additional dimension, certainly; what's more important in literary criticism terms, though, is that the act of formalising and articulating is always, to one degree or another, a *control mechanism*, and that in those extreme cases it is spectacularly noteworthy.

What follows is something I give to my Year 9 pupils every year. Don't be insulted! – I give a variant of it to sixth-formers, and if I say so myself, it is a valuable guide at any stage/age. Follow its principles and you won't go wrong.

Critical analysis of a poem/poetry: an outline strategy

1   *Choice.* Why did you choose this poem rather than another one? What makes it special to you? What might make it special to others?

2   *Theme/subject matter* (i.e. what is the poem about?). That question does *not* mean you have to spell out the obvious. If you're tackling the poetry of the First World War, it is starkly and glaringly evident that

all the poems are about the ghastliness of war, and that to point out that general observation would therefore be both useless and boring – not a great combination! What is needed instead is a more precise focus on the *particular* ghastliness or misery this or that poet addressed (e.g. disablement, boredom, madness, futility and so forth).

Further: *never explain things for the sake of it.* To take a ludicrous example, if you came across the sentence:

the cat sat on the mat,

you would both waste your readers' time and enragingly patronise them by then writing:

In this line, the writer draws our attention to the fact that a domestic feline pet is in a prone position on a small carpet.

Pompous rubbish that does nobody any good, least of all the writer!

So when *should* you explain 'what it is about'? Well, I've found this an excellent rule of thumb:

If something caused *you* difficulty, the chances are high that *your readers* will be finding it similarly problematic.

That's when you explain.

3   *How does it work/what techniques does the writer use?* This will, almost certainly, form the main body of your analysis. Look at:

- The length of the poem; length of the stanzas; regularity (or otherwise) of those stanzas. If it's a decent poem (and it is most unlikely that you will given any rubbish!), these decisions on the poet's part will be significant.
- Rhyme scheme (or lack of it). If he employs one, why did he do so? How does it assist his meaning and impact. (Or if it *doesn't*, why not?) If he includes *no* rhymes, why might that be? What's he trying to do via such an absence?
- Punctuation, flow, rhythm and line-length. Decent poets (let alone *great* ones) devote enormous attention to these things – just as much as to the words themselves. So how do such features work and assist the reader's understanding?

- Imagery, metaphors, choice of phrasing. Why does he choose this word or phrase rather than that one? Does this poetic language please or trouble/annoy you? (Don't be dismissive, but don't be too humble either: if you don't like a phrase, there's probably a good reason for it if you're being sensible.)

4 *Anything else you want to say not covered by the above.*

And finally . . .

5 *Do you like it and/or what effect does it have on you?* This is, crucially, different from Point 1 above. You might have a very good reason for having chosen poem 'x', but at the end of your study that does not necessarily mean you have to *like or approve of* poem x. In truth, it is quite unlikely that there will be a big gap between your responses to Points 1 and 5, but it is certainly possible, and if it occurs, don't worry about it: just go for it!

My final point in this specialist, yet also broadly germane, appendix is to stress that it bears out the controlling wisdom of my colleagues' top tips in Chapter 3 and a good deal of my subsequent commentary in Chapter 4. First of all, master your facts (in this particular case, what the poem is about and how the poet has deployed and structured things), and then go on to interpret it, to make it yours, to *master* it. In that respect, poetry commentary is the utter reverse of the 'airy-fairy' activity some cerebrally challenged folk declare it to be; it is as precise as the laws of Physics or the analysis of chemical compounds.

Appendix II
Instructional command verbs exercise: answers

Humanities

Account for	Explain the cause of
Analyse	Separate down into component parts and show how they interrelate with each other
Comment on	Make critical or explanatory notes/observations
Compare	Point out the differences and similarities
Contrast	Point out differences only and present result in orderly fashion
Describe	Write down the information in the right order
Discuss	Present arguments for and against the topic in question; you can also give your opinion
Evaluate	Estimate the value of, looking at positive and negative attributes
Explain	Give reasons; say 'why' rather than just define
Identify	Select features according to the question
List	Item-by-item consideration of the topic, usually presented one under the other
Outline	Give the main features or general features of a subject, omitting minor details and stressing structure
Review	Make a survey of the subject, examining it critically
Summarise	State the main features of an argument, omitting all that is only partially relevant

Science and Maths

Calculate	Obtain the answer showing all relevant working
Deduce	Show a result using known information
Determine	Obtain the answer showing all relevant working
Differentiate	Obtain the derivative of a function
Draw	Represent by means of a labelled accurate diagram or graph
Factorise	Express as a product of factors
Integrate	Obtain the integral of a function
Justify	Give a valid reason for an answer or conclusion
Plot	Mark the position of points on a diagram
Show that	Obtain the required result without the formality of proof
Sketch	Represent by means of a diagram or graph, labelled if required
Solve	Obtain the solution or root of an equation
Write down	Obtain the answer by extracting information

Appendix III
Chapter 3: Head of Department contributors, Bedford School

Michael Beale Esq.	Biology
Ian Sheldon Esq.	Chemistry
Dr Paul Arnold	Classics and Classical Civilisation
Chris Bury Esq.	Economics
Andrew Speedy Esq.	English
Dr Adrian Johnson (Director of IB)	Geography
Richard Walker Esq.	Geography
Mrs Jeanette Beale	Maths
Colin Marsh Esq.	Modern Languages
Trevor Hill Esq.	Physics
Adrian Finch Esq.	Religious Education

Notes

I Facing it

1 I shall be quoting from or referring to C.P. Snow more than once in this book, and here is a passage from arguably his finest novel, *The Masters*:

> Will, sheer stubborn will, was more effective than cunning, finesse or subtlety. Those could be a help; but the more one saw, the more one was forced to the banal conclusion that the man you wanted on your side was the man who believed without a shade of doubt that you were right.

If you can get *yourself* 'on your side' in the belief that you are right/can bring it off, you are much more likely to prosper. Snow calls that 'banal', but like many similarly everyday truths, it is a profound one.

2 The single gender is, I'm afraid, deliberate and accurate. The notion that there were no clever or talented women around until recently is, of course, preposterous; however, given the patriarchal and women-closeting nature of all Western cultures during the periods in question, women never got any real chance to prove how equally able they were to explore and develop their talent.

3 If you're one of the myriad students who have trouble spelling 'conscious' or 'conscience' correctly, it might help you to take note that the root of each word is *scio*; again, that figures, since both hinge on the concept of awareness, of *knowledge*.

4 The history of the Royal Society is a signal index of that reductive evolution. When it was founded in 1660, distinguished scholars of every kind adorned its ranks – the poet Dryden, the architect Christopher Wren, painters, composers, philosophers, mathematicians. By the twentieth century the Royal Society was exclusively made up of scientists – no less distinguished than their predecessors, to be sure, but the organisation had become a much narrower one than its founders could have imagined or, indeed, approved of.

5 That applies to independent schools too, as I well know.

6 That is emphatically not to denigrate Geography: on the contrary, it is very much a tribute to a discipline which over the last generation has become a far more vigorous, muscular and searching discipline than it was when I

was at school. Without being either frivolous or too rude, Geography then was what you did if you weren't quite good enough to do History, a kind of second division Humanity which, in the view of many, (other than geographers, of course!) lacked rigour, real focus or even point. Nowadays it is much more scientifically grounded (hence my use of 'contentious' in the main text), and significant success in it depends to quite some degree on being mathematically clued-up.

7 It also nails the National Curriculum as the massively expensive, disastrous failure that many suspected it would be from the outset.

8 In J.D. Salinger's wondrous *Catcher in the Rye*, the narrator-protagonist Holden Caulfield remarks at one point, 'All mothers are slightly insane'. I hold that to be a profound truth – and I can dispel any accusations of sexism by adding that the same thing can be said of fathers too.

2 Sorting it

1 Multiple millions of people have come out with this remark at some time or another. It is also a line from 'The Love Song of J. Alfred Prufrock' by T.S. Eliot, a poet who may be difficult, complex and open to any number of textual and spiritual interpretations, but whose verse has the kind of steely clarity that is in its way a model.

2 As furnished by Tracy Bowell and Gary Kemp in their *Critical Thinking: A Concise Guide*, p. 26.

3 'Flashpoint Zero' is Lloyds' designation for a dangerous cargo, and that's precisely what unthinking prejudice is for any student carrying it around.

4 You may be interested to learn that the puzzle featured in a 1950s Intelligence Test for UK children sitting the 11+. That exam has long been not just defunct but discredited, and one of the reasons for that discreditation hinged on the unsatisfactory, even sinister nature of those Intelligence Tests, which were pivotal in determining which children passed and which failed. The puzzle I've cited was not only academically suspect but culturally so. At this time, an increasing number of immigrant children (from the West Indies, India, Pakistan and other countries) were part of the 11+ catchment, and it ought to go without saying that it was unreasonable to assume among such candidates a governing knowledge – or any at all – of 'Key Dates in European History'. Unlike some, I would not accuse such test questions of deliberate racism; I would, however, say they were seriously wrong-headed – not least because (to return to my beginning) they confused, at a fundamental value, issues of intelligence and issues of information.

5 Stephen R. Covey, 'Inside Out', *The 7 Habits of Highly Effective People* (London: Simon & Schuster, 2004), 18.

6 Letter to Norman Iles, 17 April 1941.

7 In his magnificent *The Great Code: The Bible & Literature* (RKP, 1982), p. xv.

8 The true meaning of the Latin *educare* (to elicit, draw out) – from which, of course, the word 'education' derives.

4 Exploiting it

1 See section 5, 'Revising as you go', pp. 55–7.

2   At my school the Autumn half-term is two weeks long; I am being only semi-facetious when I say (as I not infrequently do) that one of the chief reasons for that wise generosity is to ensure that nobody dies during November.

3   Especially if that amusement hinges on sex or dirty-mindedness! I'm quite serious about that: see section 7a.

4   Paradoxically, it can be very pleasing to dwell on why you dislike something or somebody so much, just as destructive criticism is on occasion one of life's great and under-rated pleasures.

5   That is especially true in an exam, of course. Last summer I marked a set of A-level papers from a centre whose candidates had obviously received very bad planning advice. Script after script featured a hugely elaborate outline that had clearly taken at least fifteen minutes to construct; that left the candidate only forty-five minutes at most to write the actual answer. Unsurprisingly, many of them were deleteriously short, and more than a few were unfinished. In the latter instances, I tried to give as much residual credit for the undelivered plan-material as I could, but still not as much as I would have able to had the ideas in question been satisfyingly explored. In the end, you can only reward what is there, not what might have been.

6   I would add that any attempt to meet it is not only unhealthy but positively dangerous.

7   *Metalanguage* is the language we use when talking/writing about language itself. And that means *all* languages – not just all tongues but computer languages, such lexicons as the Formulaic Table in Science, mathematical formulae, and so on and so forth. Any discourse that addresses such technical terminology or code is a *metalingual* one.

8   See the Geography entry in Chapter 3, top tip 4.

9   Over- or finally indulgent use of qualifiers is an endemic flaw in my own writing, and I and my 'unofficial editors' have learnt to be ferocious about it. You'd be surprised by how much got cut from this book between first draft and final form, and here and there you might feel we've still missed the odd piece of flab!

10 *The Light and the Dark* (London: Faber & Faber, 1947). 1962 Penguin edition, 103.

11 They might even learn something: that is one of the pleasures of marking good student work.

12 Including connections with your own personality and interests; as I advised in the Mnemonics section, 'Don't look on such matters as distractions but as part of what you are as a student: get them to work *for* you.'

5   Sharpening it

1   Recently that organisation has extended its CT operation to take in A2 (Upper Sixth), and from the autumn of 2007 the subject will also be offered at AS by the AQA Board. But it is OCR's AS course which, at the time of writing, is the driving force, and as the main text indicates, its success has been phenomenal.

2   Roy van den Brink-Budgen, *Critical Thinking for Students* (Begbroke, Oxford: How To Books, 1996; 3rd Edition 2000), 17.

3　William James, *Pragmatism* (1906). The innovative university was Edinburgh.
4　Persuasively but not definitively, though: can you think of any other distinct type(s)? You'll find two more of my devising on p. 83.
5　Two questions in this area might be 'Which is Shakespeare's greatest play?' or 'What is the most attractive wallpaper?'.
6　Geography students of mine have argued that 'Russia', not 'Canada', is still the correct answer in terms of square mileage.
7　Participants in any such 'debate' – be the topic violence, sex or anything that supposedly influences behaviour – would do well to consider these remarks by Clive James:

> The assumption that ordinary people's lives could be controlled and limited by what entertained them was always too condescending to be anything but fatuous. . . . People don't get their morality from their reading matter: they bring their morality to it.
>
> ('Princess Daisy', 1993)

8　*The Deer Park* (1957).
9　The sign was invented by Robert Recorde and appeared in his *Whetstone of Witte*, 1557. He was tiring of writing out *which is the equal of* time after time, and devised the '=' symbol on the principle that 'noe 2 things can be more equal'. His device has much in common with that valuable punctuation point, the *colon*, in that both are human inventions that sharpen meaning and save a lot of time.
10　The citing of *instruction* provides one answer to the final question heading this exercise concerning 'other types of reason'. Such further possibilities as *wish fulfilment* and *desire for reassurance* have been implicit in my Commentary, and no doubt you've thought of others yourself. The field is very evidently a large one!
11　Coleridge once declared: 'No man does anything from a single motive', and experience suggests that in the overwhelming majority of instances he was right.
12　C.A. Mace, *The Psychology of Study*, p. 30. Mace wrote his book in 1932, and his style is more cautious than I think it would be were he composing the selfsame material now. So don't be fooled by the apparent moderation of 'eccentric': I have no doubt that he meant 'as near to mad as made no difference'.
13　'Obituary of Francis Crick OM', *Daily Telegraph*, Friday 30 July 2004; the italics are mine.

6　Enjoying it

1　As I've noted more than once, this is not to be confused with 'modest'.
2　You will find all such information in the 'publishing history' which is found in the first few pages of any book's text.
3　An analogous convention governs quoting from a newspaper article, as the main text illustrates shortly.
4　UCAS and other related matters are addressed in the next chapter, 'Balancing it'.

5   What is known as 'vanity publishing' is less an exception to this assertion than might appear. Yes, authors determined to get their work in print at any cost have *always* been able to do so; the word 'cost', though, is utterly the point. Private publications – be they worthy or ridiculous – have always been very expensive; as the main text points out in a moment, logging your 'vain' work on the net is immeasurably cheaper.

6   Two examples might be *De Revolutionibus Orbium Celestium*, Copernicus's 1547 proof of the nature of our planet and its orbital dependence on the sun, and Salman Rushdie's 1988 *The Satanic Verses*, which made him a hate target.

7   Which aren't all that effective, as doubtless you know. The amount of loathesomeness the net offers is something that causes concern right across the political spectrum.

8   Once again, consider the almost astonishing common ground that is the dominant feature of Chapter 3, this book's core.

9   Besides, as the old joke has it: 'Just because you're paranoid doesn't mean they're not out to get you'!

10 See Chapter 1, pp. 5–6 and Chapter 2, pp. 31–3.

11 Of course, if you're actually *allergic* to them, you need to say so at once: dutifully consuming something that will instantly make you ill is stupid. Quite apart from your own misery, your hostess will be concerned, thrown and secretly resentful: not a good overall package!

Appendix I Poetry commentary

1   The technical term for this is *mimesis*. The first four letters are the clue – imitation, physical enactment of ideas and emotions, *mimickry*. Example: in *Heart of Darkness* Joseph Conrad has a paragraph lasting 3½ pages. Normally that would be very bad writing; here, though, the length is designed to 'mimic' the huge, seemingly endless sweep of the Congo river, up which the narrator is slowly making his way. As a result, this is a hugely enabling, deepening technique, not a flaw at all.

2   'The Arrival of the Bee Box' I continue to find truly scary: it really goes right in!

Index